ENDORSEMENTS

John Kleinig invites readers to identify how shame has impacted their lives. He then engages them in a conversation, which is partly aimed at understanding shame but is mostly directed toward a single and recurring theme—Christ is our hope and our glory. As Kleinig puts it, "God's remedy for shame is not honor but glory." No quick fixes are offered, because no one plan fits for all the shamed. Rather, we are pointed to Christ, who engages with people "graciously and mercifully, respectfully and gently," and whose shame on the cross opens the pathway to glory.

—Andrew Pfeiffer, lecturer emeritus, Australian Lutheran College, Adelaide, South Australia

John Kleinig is not only an expert biblical exegete, dogmatician, and catechist, but is also, above all, a true *seelsorger*. His writings are simultaneously scholarly and accessible, a rare combination. This latest work is no exception. While tackling the central malaise of our fractured society, shame, he lavishes healing salve on broken hearts and souls in the shed blood of Christ Jesus and His merciful grace. Kleinig shows us, the walking wounded, how forgiveness and cleansing are dispensed in the sacred liturgy every Lord's Day, preparing us for the glories of the kingdom yet to come.

—Harold L. Senkbeil, author of *The Care of Souls* (Lexham, 2019) and *Dying to Live* (second edition; CPH, 2025); Waukesha, Wisconsin

FROM SHAME TO GLORY

GOD'S SURPRISING REMEDY FOR INJUSTICE & FAILURE

John W. Kleinig

To my dear sons, Timothy Kleinig and Paul Kleinig, in memory of my beloved father, Bernhard Kleinig, who had a well-tuned sense of shame and honor!

Published by Concordia Publishing House
3558 S. Jefferson Ave., St. Louis, MO 63118-3968
1-800-325-3040 • cph.org

Quotations marked WA are from the Weimar Ausgabe ("edition") of Luther's Works. *D. Martin Luthers Werke: Kritische Gesamtausgabe*. 73 vols. in 85. Weimar: Hermann Böhlau, 1883–.

Manufactured in the United States of America

1 2 3 4 5 6 7 8 9 10 35 34 33 32 31 30 29 28 27 26

CONTENTS

Preamble

Since I began to write this book on shame, something has changed in the casual conversations some people have with me. In the past, when people made polite conversation with me by asking what I was doing in my retirement and discovered I was spending much of my time writing on a religious topic, they seldom showed any interest in pursuing the discussion any further. But not now! The mere mention of shame often triggers a sudden jolt of interest and curiosity that stimulates further discussion. It is as if that word touches something largely ignored and yet significant to them. So much so that the conversation suddenly becomes personal and emotional—even, at times, confessional and spiritual. It is as if the usual social taboo on the discussion of personal issues and religious convictions has been lifted. Something important has been named. Something new is about to be discovered.

A recent encounter is a good example of this. When we offered hospitality to a homeless man last year, he wanted to know what I did for a living. After I told him that I was a retired pastor, he asked how I filled my time. I told him that I was writing a book on shame. At that, his eyes lit up. Then he sighed and said that if he were a writer, he would write a book about his life as a story of shame. He had not done that. But, as time passed, we heard his complex story of shame and its impact on him.

In these encounters, I have noticed two things that have surprised me because they were so unexpected. On the one hand, the initial social interest in the topic changed to a sense of personal engagement as soon as I distinguished shame from guilt. The insight from that distinction seemed to open the door for people to understand their experience of shame. This happened, most of all, when I touched on shame from various kinds of abuse and personal failure. On the other hand, interest in the topic was not just restricted to a particular class of people, such as churchgoers or sexually abused women. It extended across the board from young to old, from Christians to atheists, from the well-educated to people with little education, and it included people of both sexes, all ethnicities, all social classes, and all occupations.

Even though the reasons for their personal interest in shame differed from person to person, case to case, and context to context, everybody seemed to stand on common ground with a similar sense about shame. Even so, despite all similarities, it was hard to generalize about their actual experience of shame, apart from its social orientation and its connection with the identity of each person. I have discovered that shame is so hard to pin down because it is so personal. Our sense of shame has to do with who we are, our unique identity despite our common humanity. We are all prone to shame in a different way, because each of us has been made as a unique person in God's image.

As I have been writing this book, I have been uncertain how to tackle the issue of shame respectfully and sensitively, in its full personal complexity, without sounding as if I were an expert on it, when my knowledge and awareness of it has come largely from my own experience as a person and a pastor. I have therefore run the first chapter of the book past people who I know well, to get feedback from them. In most cases, the response has been that my reflections have, as I had hoped, opened up the topic for them. It named something significant that had been previously unnamed and unexplained, something that they had not really noticed, let alone understood. It triggered a chain of reflection on shame and their own experience of it.

Let me mention just one recent instance of this. A few weeks ago, I shared the first chapter of this book with a young fellow pastor. After reading it, he said the topic of shame kept cropping up for him over and over again. In a short span of time, it came up in three different situations. First, he brought it up rather tentatively in a Bible study on 2 Timothy 1:1–14, where Paul tells young Pastor Timothy that, like Paul in prison in Rome, he had no reason to be ashamed of Jesus or of suffering for the Gospel. Prompted by what he had read, this pastor spoke about being shamed and asked why Timothy would be ashamed of his connection with Jesus and Paul. The Bible study led to an animated discussion of the participants' own experiences of shame from being rejected by friends and family for their convictions and commitment to God's Word. In this, they found that it was helpful to distinguish wrongful, misplaced shame from appropriate shame for doing something wrong or failing to fulfill a duty.

After that, the pastor visited a conscientious young man who was plagued with a bad conscience from his repeated failure to keep God's Law. The pastor was able to help the young man by distinguishing his guilt—with the need for confession and absolution—from his failure to meet the impossible expectations that he had set for himself. The pastor helped the young man to turn his attention away from himself and his self-esteem to Jesus, to ask Him to take away his shame as well as his guilt.

Then, soon after that, the pastor met with a woman who had left her abusive husband. Hiding behind a pious front, the husband had abused her emotionally for twenty years. Even though she had, with God's help, forgiven him, she still felt guilty, because she still felt as deeply hurt as ever by his abuse and could not forget how badly he had wounded her. The pastor suggested that her "guilt" could, in fact, be the shame that he had put on her by belittling and abusing her. That remark hit home for her and brought her to tears of relief. By naming her shame and distinguishing it from guilt, the pastor was able to help the woman to join with him in prayer that God would take away her shame and set her free from the deep, toxic hurt of her abuse by her husband.

These three cases deal with three different, common experiences of shame and its impact on the conscience. In each case, the pastor named the shame by distinguishing it from guilt.

My hope for you, as you read and study this book, is that it will help you to name the shame that you have experienced but may not yet have understood—or only partly understood, or even misunderstood by confusing it with guilt—and will encourage you to look for relief from its burden and its impact on you.

But before you do that, I would invite you to consider whether, when, and how you yourself have been shamed, and how that has affected you. Begin where you are and discover where that takes you as you read this book.

CHAPTER ONE

Naming Shame

The unjust knows no shame.

(Zephaniah 3:5)

If only I were such a blameless person that I would be rightly honored and admired because there was nothing wrong with either me or those who lived with me. I would then have nothing to hide and be quite happy to be openly seen as I am in body, soul, and spirit. Like Adam and Eve, I could be fully seen but not at all ashamed (Genesis 2:25). I would be rightly shameless.

We all know that this is an impossible dream. No matter how hard we try, we cannot change ourselves and our society so completely that we would have no need to be ashamed of ourselves and no longer be afraid that we would ever be shamed. In fact, the story of humanity seems to be an endless story of shame from generation to generation, shame that may be alleviated but is never eradicated.

Yet our lives need not end in disillusionment and disappointment. There is another story, a love story, the wonderful story of the promise of divine intervention and its amazing fulfillment. Its unexpected turn from shame to glory is summed up by Paul in Ephesians 5:25–27: "Christ loved the church and gave Himself up for her, that He might sanctify her, having cleansed her by the washing of water with the word, so that He might present the church to Himself in splendor, without spot or wrinkle or any such thing, that she might be holy and without blemish." God's Son became a man and sacrificed Himself for us and the whole church to make us spotless and splendid, pure and holy in His sight. He has set us free from our guilt and shame by washing us completely clean in Baptism. Through faith in Him, we are now blameless and beyond reproach (Colossians 1:22). Through Him, we now no longer have any reason to be ashamed of ourselves because He covers us with His purity and holiness.

A Journey of Discovery

It has taken me a long time to recognize what shame is and how it works; it has taken me even longer to realize how it has affected me in myself as well as in my relationship with others and God. Even though I have always felt its impact, mostly vaguely and sometimes acutely, I have not known what to make of it and how to deal with it. It lurks there in me and around me, unrecognized and unacknowledged, hidden in plain sight. Even though I don't know why, I fear public shaming as one of the worst things that could ever happen to me.

Despite my haunting sense of shame, I have been unable to deal with it for two main reasons. On the one hand, because shame has affected me psychologically, I have regarded it as little more than a negative emotional state that calls for better self-understanding to minimize its damage and, if that does not work, treatment by a trained cognitive therapist. On the other hand, because shame is often associated with guilt and is similar in its effects, I have equated shame with guilt, both morally and theologically. That has enabled me to dismiss its effect without dealing with the reasons for it or finding a remedy for it. So, for example, when I was angry with people who had slandered me, I told myself that I needed to seek forgiveness from God for feeling angry with them and to forgive them for what they had done. But that did not deal with the shame they had inflicted on me. It did not identify the reason I felt such acute shame, nor did it release me from its grip. The hurt and anger from the words or actions remained.

My misunderstanding of shame and my confusion of shame with guilt have hampered me in my journey of emotional and spiritual discovery. They have prevented me from making sense of myself and my own experience. They have also stopped me from recognizing how I have shamed other people and have made it harder for me to work with people whom I have shamed. They have made me a slow learner, even though the fallout from shame was there for me to see in myself and the people around me. My misjudgment of myself has led me to misjudge others. It is a bit like what Jesus warns us about in Matthew 7:1–5. I could not see the speck in the eye of my brother, or sister, because I had a plank in my own eye. That plank prevented me from noticing what the Bible had to say about shame and helping people who had been shamed.

Broadly speaking, there have been three stages of gradual growth in my understanding of shame. From these, I have gained some key insights into shame's social context, cultural formation, and spiritual dimension.

The first foundational stage in my understanding of shame came from my own social background. On both sides of my family, I belong to an ethnic minority here in Australia that has struggled to survive in an alien environment among a social majority that has disadvantaged and even persecuted us. My family belongs to a conservative Lutheran community of migrants who were Wends. Also known as Sorbs, Wends were a Slavic tribal group with its homeland east of the River Elbe on the border between present-day Germany and Poland. In the late Middle Ages, the Wends were taken over by German feudal overlords who treated them with disdain as uncivilized peasants and forced assimilation on them. But the Wends survived because their Lutheran heritage helped them to maintain their language, culture, and identity. In the early nineteenth century, many Wends migrated to Australia to escape religious discrimination and persecution in Prussia. Sadly, in Australia, they were identified with the German Lutheran settlers in South Australia during the two world wars and were persecuted along with them. The Wends in Australia suffered all kinds of public shaming because they were held to be German migrants.

Even though I grew up after the Second World War, I, like my Irish Catholic friends, was frequently reminded of my ambiguous status as a member of a different religious, ethnic community—a close-knit community that did not share the customs and values of the dominant English, Protestant majority who used the threat of shame to force assimilation as the price for social acceptance.

By their disapproval, they tried to make us feel ashamed of our ethnic identity and religious affiliation. Many Lutherans tried to remove their shame by changing their surnames and joining other "socially respectable" religious denominations. Even though I have tried to dismiss its significance, this record of public disapproval has left its mark on me. It has made me aware that my sense of shame has more to do with my social status than who I actually am and how I feel about myself.

The second stage in my cultural understanding of shame was triggered by my interaction with some Aboriginal Lutheran students from a remote, traditional community in North Queensland whom I prepared for confirmation as a college chaplain early in my ministry at a secondary boarding school in Brisbane. On a number of occasions, I overheard them mutter one to another, "Shame job!" and "No shame!" I eventually learned that the former exclamation was a warning to one of them about doing something that would be shameful and single them out for the disapproval of their fellow students. In contrast, the other exclamation was an assurance that what one of them had said or done had not or would not incur shame. These remarks stimulated me to investigate the place that respect and shame had in their culture. I discovered that they had an elaborate etiquette to avoid shaming others and to deal with shame when it occurred. So, for example, when I directed a question to a girl, the girl next to her would answer it. The second girl "covered" for the first so that she would not lose face by giving the wrong answer. This and many other similar experiences have taught me much about shame and have helped me to understand its social significance.

The third decisive stage in my theological understanding of shame was stimulated by my pastoral care of people who had been severely abused: first, those who had been victims of sexual abuse, and then those who had been victims of other kinds of abuse. As I listened to these people, I discovered that, like the guilt from sin, the shame from abuse had given them a bad conscience. They felt unworthy and out of place in God's presence. No matter how much they tried, they could not pray. They stayed away from church and felt that they should not receive Holy Communion. Above all else, they felt unclean before God and condemned by Him. But they did not really know why. They thought that they must have done something wrong, because they felt so bad about themselves. They wondered whether they felt unworthy because they had done something wrong or whether God disapproved of them because they could not forgive those who had abused them. In my pastoral care of these people, I therefore learned to name shame as the main reason for their distress. I also learned to distinguish the shame that they felt as a result of the abuse they had experienced from the guilt they felt for other reasons, such as their desire for revenge.

Even though my awareness of shame has come from my personal experience, this book is not my story of its discovery. It is not about me at all. Rather, it is the story of God's help for all of us in our shame. In this book, I want to recall what God's Word teaches us about the origin of shame, its use and abuse, its effects and the fallout from it, and, most of all, about God's diagnosis of it and remedy for it. Even though shame is immensely complex and very different in different contexts, the message of the Bible is quite simple. Like the Aboriginal students I taught long ago, God tells each of you who trust in Jesus, "No shame!" as He reaches out to free you from temporal and eternal shame. His promise is that whoever believes in Jesus will not be put to shame (Romans 9:33; 10:11; 1 Peter 2:6).

The Nature of Shame

Like much of human behavior, shame is hard to define. Even though it affects us in all parts of our life—physically and socially, mentally and emotionally, personally and spiritually—we can't pin it down and tell exactly what it is. We can gauge its complexity from the way we speak about it. So, for example, we use the word *shame* to describe the following interrelated things:

- Physical shyness, modesty, reticence, and self-concealment
- Awareness of what is socially dishonorable, unpresentable, and unacceptable
- Discomfort and pain that is felt about something dishonorable and unacceptable in ourselves and others
- Disappointment from misplaced confidence in a person or a cause
- Embarrassment at public exposure and critical evaluation
- Hypersensitivity to censure and unjust rejection

- Abusive, hurtful acts by which others show their disapproval and rejection of us
- Social disgrace and reproach that results from public disapproval and rejection
- The effect of unjust disapproval and disgrace on how we feel about ourselves and our sense of worth
- The feeling of personal worthlessness and failure

Thus the same word covers a wide range of different and yet related personal things. It is hard to distinguish these from one another because they all describe what happens at the intersection of our private self-consciousness and our public status.

In simple terms, shame is the opposite of honor. Both are conferred and confirmed by others in the court of public opinion, a helpful modern term that describes their resemblance to the judgment of people in a court of law, which either vindicates or condemns them. The problem is that this "court" operates without an impartial, duly-authorized judge and objective code of law. The people who bring charges also belong to the jury that judges and sentences, and to the penal system that carries out the sentence. And that is what makes our sense of shame so precarious and uncertain.

While shame is much like guilt in some circumstances, it also differs significantly from it. I am guilty when I have done something wrong, done something that damages my relationship with others and God. Guilt comes from doing evil deeds, from breaking the law, whether it be the moral law or God's Law. My guilty conscience tells me that an evil deed needs to be rectified before the breach in a relationship can be restored. The opposite of guilt is innocence. Guilty people seek to justify themselves by what they do and wish to be justified by the positive verdict of others on them.

In contrast with guilt, which makes me feel bad about what I have done, shame makes me see myself in a negative light, so that I regard myself as a bad person. When I am ashamed, I feel that I have failed as a person; I realize that there is something wrong with me; I feel that I am bad, a loser, or someone with no hope; I am not the person I should be or, even, that I would like to be. At its worst, shame discredits and disables me; it makes me feel unacceptable and insignificant, useless and worthless. So when I am shamed, I want to be vindicated.

The opposite of shame is honor. The shame that I feel is connected with my sense of self, my standing with others, my public face and acceptability, my reputation and social standing, the respect that I have or do not have in my community. It makes me aware of social approval and disapproval. With shame comes the loss of face, of how I present myself in public. While the approval of my colleagues honors me, their disapproval shames me.

My feeling that I am acceptable is damaged, diminished, and destroyed by five main causes: my wrongdoing to others, their abuse of me, my failure to be the person I would like to be or should be, my unacceptable status, and my self-deception. First, I feel guilty and ashamed of myself when I have done something wrong toward others, like stealing something that belongs to someone else. Second, I feel ashamed of myself when something bad is done to me, such as when I have been sexually abused or bullied or slandered. Third, I feel ashamed of myself when I let myself and others down, such as if I fail an exam, lose my job, become bankrupt, or get divorced. Fourth, I feel ashamed of myself when I suffer disrespect for who I am or from what I am—my appearance or parentage, my race or ethnicity, my deficiencies and disabilities, my occupation or lack of employment, my sexual or marital status, my religious adherence or political convictions, and so on. Fifth, I am ashamed of myself when I realize that I have built my sense of self and my life on an idol, something unreal and untrue, a delusion, like a false ideology or a false creed with its set of wrong beliefs about the world, myself, and God.

Even though guilt and shame both affect us emotionally, shame is also felt physically, so much so that, like physical pain, it seems to be a physical sensation located in some parts of the body. Thus, when I am shamed, I blush from the rush of blood to my face that heats my cheeks. I also drop my face and avoid direct eye contact with other people for fear of their gaze and what it tells about their attitude toward me. I also close the posture of my body by lowering my head and dropping my shoulders, so that my hands and whole body become slack and withdrawn in a defensive demeanor. But those reactions can also turn from physical disengagement to a defiant posture and a heated sense of aggressive confrontation. We react to shame by flight from it or fight with those who have shamed us; this is often accompanied by a rush of adrenaline. Whatever the case, shame is as physical as it is emotional. It is a symptom of our personal and social embodiment.

Unlike guilt, shame is shared by others in many instances. While we as individuals feel guilty when we have done something wrong, we as a community are ashamed when our leaders or compatriots have done something shameful. Think of the shame of parents and a whole family when a child commits a crime or becomes an addict. Think of the shame of a sports team when its captain violates the rules of the game. Think of the shame of a congregation or a denomination when one of its leaders is found guilty of sexual impropriety or child abuse. Think of the shame of citizens when their leaders are found guilty of gross negligence, severe corruption, or a blatant crime. Think of the shame of a nation such as the United States from the approval of slavery by their ancestors, or Australia from the mistreatment of its original inhabitants. Think of the shame that many of us feel about the legalization of abortion and euthanasia. In all these cases, people are ashamed of something bad that they themselves have not done. They bear and share a common sense of shame. They suffer from shame by their association with others who have done something shameful. While guilt is personal, shame is also communal, social, and national. A whole community may also be shamed by institutional injustice and systemic oppression.

Thus, in the Old Testament, God's people were put to shame by what their leaders did. They were all shamed when their national enemies defeated them in battle, enslaved their captured soldiers as prisoners of war, deported their leaders, occupied their land, and oppressed its remaining inhabitants. And even worse than that, they were put to shame by their triumphant enemies, who taunted them and their God for their impotence and inability to defend themselves.

Like guilt, shame is not in itself a bad thing. A healthy sense of shame is an essential part of life for people in a well-ordered, harmonious community. It is associated with their proper sensitivity to the people around them in their interaction with them and their respect for them. It has to do with the decency and courtesy that is shown in politeness and good manners. It guards their inner self, their self-esteem, and assures them of their respectability, their place in society. But despite the riches of our English vocabulary, we do not have a word for this good sense of shame and its proper use. The best noun that I know is the old-fashioned word *modesty* as the honest self-awareness by which we do not make too much or too little of ourselves and our social status. The verb that best describes a good use of shaming is *admonish*. It is used for wise, respectful instruction in constructive behavior and the kind, gentle correction of destructive activity.[1] It encourages what is consistent with the welfare of a person and warns against the damage done by disrespectfulness.

A positive sense of shame is divinely given, God's good gift to us by our creation in His image, something latent and inherent in our humanity. Positively speaking, it is closely associated with the personal modesty and humility that comes from the awareness of our worth with God and dependence on Him for our identity. It shields our personal integrity and protects our honor. So, shame

1 See the use of the Greek verb νουθετέω (admonish) by Paul in Acts 20:31; Romans 15:14; 1 Corinthians 4:14; Colossians 1:28; 3:16; 1 Thessalonians 5:12, 14; 2 Thessalonians 3:15; and its noun νουθεσία (admonition) in 1 Corinthians 10:11; Ephesians 6:4; Titus 3:10.

and honor belong together; they correspond with each other, like the two sides of the same coin. Shame shows us how God sees our shortcomings. As such, it turns on us when we reject Him. Since we were meant to live in community with one another and with Him, shame shows us that we, like Adam and Eve, have fallen out with Him and are far from His glory; we become ashamed of ourselves and cover up before God and one another because we do not measure up to God's expectation of us. Thus, shame is an index of our standing with others and God.

A New Challenge

Shame is at work all around us. Even though it is often unacknowledged, it motivates all of us personally and socially, because we all live in community together. It is at play everywhere people work together and personally interact. It is most evident in public life and politics.

Let me mention two common instances of it. We see it at work in the pressure that teenagers feel from their peers as they move away from their families in search of their place in an adult world. Since they are uncertain about themselves and their worth, they crave approval from others their age. For them, the price of recognition and acceptance in their social circle is conformity to a dominant group, with its behavior, dress, and values. Those who do not join in with it are disparaged and shunned. They are shamed into acquiescence and compliance. Peer group leaders manipulate their followers to gain and retain power over them. Since the members of the group wish to gain peer acceptance and approval, they risk greater but later shame to avoid the smaller but present shame from ridicule and rejection.

We see it too in our need to find a place for ourselves in society, whether it be at school, work, sport, or anywhere else. Our place, our standing, depends largely on the approval of the leaders, the people in charge who assess us and our performance, the managers who have the power to reward us and promote us. They use our desire for recognition and our fear of shame to motivate us. Our reputation is also tested and confirmed by interaction with our colleagues. There we learn proper social intelligence and respectful behavior. There we discover how to disagree with others without belittling them. There we come to appreciate the value of honest loyalty and the protection provided by others who cover for us. There the healthy interplay of honor and shame shapes us and produces a positive sense of shame through acceptance and approval.

Even though the use of shame to produce social cooperation and encourage personal compliance is nothing new, it has been adapted and reshaped by the internet via cellphones and other digital devices. This visual and verbal means of interaction and communication has been widely adopted, for both better and worse, by what is now called social media. So, for example, during the COVID-19 pandemic, I was able to stay in touch with people around the world and deliver lectures to many different groups via Zoom without actually visiting them.

At its worst, social media has provided a new powerful weapon for politicians, culture warriors, and social activists who use it to attack and ridicule their opponents with impunity. Think of how political candidates for public office in the United States and elsewhere have ridiculed their rivals and defamed them with their postings and tweets. Also think of the Me Too movement, with its tactic of naming and shaming real or alleged male sexual offenders.

The use of social media has shown how pervasive the fear of being shamed is in our society and how desperate people are for attention and significance, recognition and approval. Consider the widespread appeal and surprising success of Facebook. It is aptly named because it offers its users a public "face" with its selfie pictures and personal postings. Yet its appeal goes well beyond mere recognition. By its solicitation of likes and dislikes, it establishes a virtual community of friends and followers. But it also plays on the deep-seated fear of disapproval by cancellation and rejection by "unfriending." It has created a digital culture that is based on honor and shame.

The influence of social media has alerted us to the power of shame. It has shown us how public shaming damages people. Think, for example, of the young people who have been driven to suicide by ridicule and visual caricatures of their physical appearance! Yet despite the crude exploitation of shame to damage vulnerable people, we should not conclude that our sense of shame is bad. It is not something that we need to eliminate if we want to thrive and live well with other people. When it works as it should, shame defends our honor and protects us from the peril of shamelessness.

Shamelessness

A healthy sense of shame is an invaluable asset. It is God's good gift to us by our creation in His image for fellowship with Him and one another. It is latent in our humanity. It is an essential aspect of our self-consciousness. Yet, like all God's good gifts, it can be mistaken and misused. If it functions properly, it is useful and helpful, like a fire alarm or a stomachache. It is essential to our personal and spiritual health and growth. We cannot live at peace without it, because it shows us how we are regarded by others and God. It shows us that our sense of self and our worth depends on God and His approval of us. Just as our guilt tells us that we have done something wrong, our shame tells us that there is something wrong with us, like Bartimaeus with his blindness (Mark 10:46–52) and the woman with her pollution by the continuous menstrual discharge of blood (Luke 8:43–48).

If we had no sense of shame, we would be largely insensitive to others and unaware of what is required from us in our relationship with them. We would, in fact, be narcissistic sociopaths with no capacity for friendship and love. A sense of shame, like our desire for approval, is part and parcel of our creation for life in community with others. Just as we would be foolish to rid ourselves of people who have hurt us, so we would be even more foolish to eliminate our sense of shame and refuse to learn from it. We do not need to free ourselves from shame but to have it refined so that broken relationships can be restored. Shame is meant to be a good friend, not a bad enemy.

I admit that the positive value of shame may be rather hard to grasp. It is, I think, best understood by its contrast with the destructive impact of shamelessness. That is much worse than the hurt we suffer from the most shameful kinds of abuse and the worst kinds of failure. Eliminating our sense of shame would be like overcoming pain by desensitizing our nervous system.

Through the prophet Jeremiah, God compares His bride, the city of Jerusalem, to a brazen prostitute with this sad lament in 3:3: "You have the forehead of a whore; you refuse to be ashamed." Then a little later, in 8:8–12, He has this to say about the careless shamelessness of its religious leaders:

> 8 How can you say, "We are wise,
> and the law of the LORD is with us"?
> But behold, the lying pen of the scribes
> has made it into a lie.
> 9 The wise men shall be put to shame;
> they shall be dismayed and taken;
> behold, they have rejected the word of the LORD,
> so what wisdom is in them?
> 10 Therefore I will give their wives to others
> and their fields to conquerors,
> because from the least to the greatest
> everyone is greedy for unjust gain;
> from prophet to priest,
> everyone deals falsely.
> 11 They have healed the wound of My people lightly,
> saying, "Peace, peace,"

when there is no peace.
*12*Were they ashamed when they committed abomination?[2]
No, they were not at all ashamed;
they did not know how to blush.[3]

Shame has to do with our face-to-face interaction with the people around us. It is on display physically with our faces and what they communicate visually by attention and reaction to other people. In public, we read one another's faces, and those faces often tell us much more than what their owners say verbally. Shame is shown by how we look at others and how we react when others look at us. Thus, when we are ashamed, we either avoid eye contact with people or else blush with embarrassment at their gaze. We are ashamed to be seen by them. We can also, if we wish, cover our shame by putting on a brazen face that defies censure and disapproval. That is what shameless people do with their personal demeanor, which says in effect, "I don't care what you think of me, because you don't count for me at all."

Jeremiah reads the faces of the religious leaders in Jerusalem—the scribes, priests, and prophets who ridicule him and reject what God says to them through him. He sees that they no longer know how to blush because they have switched off their ears to God's voice and shut their hearts to His Law because it has exposed their sin. They therefore use God's Word to justify their sin and excuse their shamelessness. Their deliberate misapplication and distortion of God's Word desensitizes them spiritually, emotionally, and

2 In Jeremiah 23:14, God laments that the prophets in Jerusalem not only justified their own adultery but also excused the evildoing of the people by their false teaching.

3 Jeremiah 8:10b–12 recalls 6:13–15.

physically, so much so that they no longer know how to blush. They have lost their physical and mental, moral and spiritual compass.

Their descent into shamelessness and the fallout from it stemmed not from their ignorance of God's Law but from their familiarity with it. In their greed for assets and wealth, they abused their God-given status in order to cheat their poor, disadvantaged fellow citizens and manipulate the courts of law to escape punishment for what they had done. They used their knowledge of God's Law to justify their unjust exploitation and excuse their perversion of justice. Then they covered up their ungodly self-deception by using God's Word to preach false peace to other evildoers rather than by healing through repentance and reliance on His pardon.

They embraced three kinds of shamelessness. First, they did what they knew was shameful in God's eyes. Then they twisted God's Word to excuse their wrongdoing and justify their actions to themselves and others. Then, last and worst, they used their expertise and prestige to excuse and sanction the sins of others. By their personal shamelessness, they promoted even worse public shamelessness. This shamelessness was so ingrained that God announces that, as His last resort for them, He will put them to shame by the conquest of Jerusalem and their deportation by its conquerors as prisoners of war far from their homeland.

A Dark Maze

Like most other personal matters, shame needs to be understood specifically rather than abstractly, particularly rather than generally. It needs to be distinguished from similar, related things, like depression or low self-esteem, by being named accurately in its actual social context. But that is a hard thing for us to do. For me personally, I know it is hard because my sense of shame is so much a part of me as a whole person and my whole life. It is so close to me that I can't see it properly, like the birthmarks on my back. It is very much like my face, which I can see only in parts, like my nose, or in a blurry outline. Like a person who is blind, I need to have it named by others to see it for myself.

All too often, shame makes me feel like I am in a dark maze in which I try to find my way by myself at night with the help of a little candle but without a map or any signposts. I can see where I am, but I don't know where that is in the whole maze. I don't know how to find my way through it, because there are so many false paths and dead ends. Like getting lost in a maze, my understanding of shame is rather confused and confusing for three mains reasons.

The first reason for confusion is social and cultural. While shame is at work in all societies, some societies are better equipped culturally to identify it and deal with it, such as the traditional Aboriginal people in Australia that I mentioned earlier. Sociologists call these "shame cultures," and these include such people as the tribal communities in Africa or the traditional monarchy of Japan. These are in contrast with "guilt cultures," like western European societies with their Protestant heritage. Each of these cultures has its own social mentality and moral code of conduct that makes them understand the same things differently from other cultures. So people like me with my religious heritage usually assess wrongdoing legally, according to innocence or guilt, rather than socially, according to honor and shame. We therefore are often ill-equipped mentally and culturally to handle shame, because our culture obscures it by equating it with guilt or the loss of personal self-esteem. So even when we name it, we don't name it correctly. We are, by and large, blind to our own sense of shame, even when we are experts at shaming people.

The second reason for confusion is personal. Even though we can usually name the people who have shamed us, we find it hard to see and understand shame properly in our own behavior, because it has to do with our own being, our personal identity, our souls, our whole sense of self as persons. Shaming attacks us personally and treats us as if we were nonentities, nameless nobodies. It threatens to cancel me, to negate me as a person. Even if the injury is not consciously intended, that is how it feels when I am uncertain about myself and my status. So, the more uncertain I am about myself and my own worth, the more demeaning, devastating, and destructive shaming is. Unless I have a secure sense of self, shaming presents an existential threat to me by calling into question my right to exist. The outer attacks on me trigger an ongoing inner conflict in me, a desperate battle to maintain my sense of worth and vindicate myself in the face of rejection and condemnation. And that clouds my perception and distorts my judgment.

The third reason for confusion is emotional. The experience of shame evokes some powerful and toxic human emotions, such as indignation, anger, and rage against an injustice; hostility, hatred, malice, spite, and vindictiveness against the offender; and bitterness, resentment, and self-reproach from the offense. And these emotions are expressed to an extreme degree of intensity—so much so that the emotional reaction to the offense seems to be disproportionate, exaggerated, and unwarranted to the onlooker. Yet that is how it is for a shamed person. The deeper the personal hurt and the worse the injustice, the more extreme the emotional fallout from the offense.

When these emotions are bottled up and repressed, as they usually are, they feed on one another and increase in their intensity, like water in a pressure cooker, until they explode. Then all that is needed is the right trigger for them to erupt in a torrent of verbal abuse and an outburst of physical violence. While the outburst can be triggered by anybody at hand, it is focused in general on all those who have shamed the person and, in particular, on the worst offender, who somehow embodies the hurt. As we so often see in the Psalms, they are "my enemies" and the worst of them is "the enemy." So the emotional impact of unjust abuse makes it hard to name the shame calmly and dispassionately or to distinguish person from person and case from case, the cause of each incident from its outcome, and the effect of the worst offenses from their total damage. It is all too much, all too confused and confusing, to be named by dispassionate analysis and explanation. The best shamed people can do is to say how they feel, and why, to a patient, sympathetic, compassionate listener who encourages them to name the shame by pouring out their hearts emotionally and graphically, as is done in the Psalms.

The Hope of Glory

I am writing this book at a time when the topic of shame is suddenly and surprisingly on the agenda in the public domain in countries like Australia and the United States. It has in the past received scant attention in the Western world and been largely ignored in its churches. But now it is evident in many different ways and many different places, from the family to the workplace, schools to politics, the church to the courts of law, the arts to television, and elsewhere. There are many reasons for this, but I will not explore them here, and I am ill-equipped to explore them because I am not a psychologist or a sociologist or a cultural analyst but a pastor and theologian.

My aim is to help you examine your experience of shame, understand it better, and discover how your sense of shame is bound up with who you are. I also want to encourage you to look for something greater and far better than your honor and self-esteem. My purpose is summed up in two simple phrases from the apostle Paul in Colossians 1:27: "the riches of the glory"[4] and "the hope of glory."[5] This is reflected in the title of this book. I had originally intended to write about shame and honor. But that has changed with my surprising discovery that God's remedy for shame is not honor but glory. It is not His affirmation of me as I am in myself but as I am as His child and heir in Jesus. It is not His restoration of my honor but my participation in His glory through my union with Him.

4 See also Romans 9:23; Ephesians 1:18; 3:16; Philippians 4:19.

5 See also Romans 5:2.

Questions for Reflection and Discussion

1. Is there anything in this chapter that you would like to discuss?

2. What recent examples of public shaming have you noticed?

3. In what ways have you or someone close to you been severely damaged by shame? How?

4. Reflect on the difference between shame and guilt, and discuss why it is helpful to make this distinction.

5. In what ways is our sense of shame beneficial to us in our relationship with others and God?

6. Which emotions increase our shame? Which emotions cloud our understanding of it? How?

CHAPTER TWO

Origin and Damage Control

O men,[6] how long shall my honor
be turned into shame?

(Psalm 4:2)

Shaming affects our identity. When we are shamed, our sense of self is threatened because shame makes us question who we are. It also affects how others regard us. Shame has to do with our inner being, our private sense of self, which is mostly hidden from public view but is always in play. And that is why we are so perplexed by our shame and why we find it hard to know what to make of it.

So, for example, how should I react when I am ridiculed for my considered skepticism about vaccination against COVID-19, or criticized for my German Lutheran heritage when I reckon that I should be proud of it? Have I done something wrong? Or is there something wrong with me? Or do my critics try to damage my reputation and bolster their own status at my expense by shaming me? How do these charges differ from the accusation that I have mistreated someone in my congregation? In sum, why am I so vexed by the shame that I experience?

6 Literally, "you children of Adam."

The experts, such as psychologists and sociologists, seem to be just as perplexed as I am by the power of shame and the fallout from it. They disagree on its origin and nature, but most consider that it has no positive personal value. They usually understand it as a negative emotion and harmful notion, like guilt, something so damaging and destructive that it needs to be disregarded or repudiated. As for its origin, they regard it dismissively as a neurotic reaction to repressed sexuality or an unfortunate remnant of primitive beliefs and religious superstitions that will gradually disappear as people become more enlightened.

But that has not happened in the Western world. Instead, shame has staged an unexpected comeback in the public domain. The recognition of its powerful resurgence has triggered a positive reevaluation of it as an instrument of social cohesion, something necessary for good social order and the mutually beneficial interaction of people with one another. If you want to find out more about this trend, look up this topic on Google. There you will discover a new evolutionary account of shame as a social basis for the survival of a community, the impetus for its productive operation, and the use of public approval as the social reward for the orderly cooperation of its members with one another for the benefit of the whole community.

No matter how fashionable these theories may be, they do not really account for the origin of shame, its ambiguity as both beneficial and detrimental, and its proper management, because they all consider it either as a natural physical mechanism or as a human social construct. They cannot explain why primates—the animals who are most like human beings—do not appear to experience shame as we do. Nor do they explain why something so beneficial for human life can have such a negative impact on human beings.

There is, in truth, much that is simply perplexing about shame. Why are we so prone to shame? Why are we so embarrassed by the public exposure of our naked bodies or some parts of them? What kinds of treatment shame us, and why? Why do we feel shamed or honored by what people say of us? Why does shaming damage people so badly, and for so long? Would we be better off if we were completely insensitive and immune to shame? Why do we find it so hard to say what shame is, even though we have all experienced it in so many ways? So many questions and so few answers!

For me to find my way through the dim light that envelops me when I feel ashamed, I need to have a true sense of my own identity and relate my shame to it. I need to be able to distinguish between the shame of my guilt from my own wrongdoing and the shame from my humiliation from the abuse that I have experienced. Above all else, I need practical protection from injustice and the abuse of power.

In my confusion and perplexity, the Old Testament of the Bible gives me a nuanced, multidimensional religious account of shame that does justice to its complex origin, offers God's help for its management, and provides the prospect of eventual deliverance from it by Him. The foundation for that is set out in the story of God's creation of humanity and its fall in Genesis 1–3.

Identity and Shame

Shame has to do with our identity, our selfhood, our sense of self. There is general agreement on that from those who have studied what it is and how it works. We become aware of it and feel it when our sense of self is threatened and attacked in some way.

Shame works much like our autonomic nervous system, which triggers a physical, emotional response to a physical threat to our body. When we are abused, it tells us that our sense of self is in danger. It triggers a set of self-protective reactions that are both physical and emotional, such as a fearful "flight" to escape further damage, a panic-stricken "freeze" in the face of danger, and an angry "fight back" in a counterattack against it. Its obvious purpose is to defend what is most precious and vital to us: our identity, our sense of self, and our worth, our awareness—however vague or dim—of who we are rather than just what we are. Our whole life is damaged if that is damaged. Something vital to us is put to death if that is destroyed. At least, that is how it feels to us. If we are worthless, our life is no longer worth living. We lose the will to live because we feel that we have lost the right to live.

You may have noticed that I have been using *identity* as the word to describe what I mean by our sense of self. It is an old word that is now being used in a new way for what we have no other generally accepted current name. It refers to what used to be called our *soul*, the traditional term for human beings as animate persons who relate to one another and to God personally with their whole being. But that use of *soul* is no longer in common use. It is now taken as something separate from the body and identified with the self-conscious mind rather than with who we are as whole persons, whether we are awake or asleep, conscious or unconscious.

In the past, *identity* was a word that described two objective things about people: that they remained the same persons with the same names throughout their lives and that they had the same social status that confirmed their separate existence as such. For better or worse, *identity* now also refers to our subjective sense of self and our worth as persons with a unique status. This is what makes us prone to shame in all its guises, for our shame has to do with our identity and the consequent social status, personal worth, and public respect that it entails.

The story of God's creation of our primeval parents gives us a surprising account of our innate identity with its high status and great worth as God's amazing gift to every human being. He decided to confer it on all people before He created them. It had to do with why He created them. He conferred it on them when He made them. Thus, in Genesis 1:26, we hear how God said, "Let Us make man in Our image, after Our likeness." Then, in the next verse, we have this report of its enactment:

> So God created man[7] in His own image,
> in the image of God He created him;
> male and female[8] He created them.[9]

7 The wording of this little poem reflects the use of the same Hebrew word, *adam*, to refer specifically to a male person, such as Adam, and inclusively as a term for mankind, all humanity.

8 In Hebrew, these terms are used to refer to both the sex and gender of people and animals.

9 This radical declaration stands in sharp contrast to the teaching of some religions in the ancient world that a male king, such as Pharaoh in Egypt, was the image of the supreme god or else made like him by adoption at his coronation.

These three carefully crafted statements disclose the identity and status of all people God has created.[10] They obtain their identity from Him and His creation of them, their true identity with its real status and real sense of worth.

Their identity has two basic dimensions to it: one by their standing with God and the other by their standing with the opposite sex. Both of these are marked by likeness and unlikeness, similarity and dissimilarity. These states of being are the two God-given foundations for their personal, human identity. They are more inherent to all people than their DNA, even after their fall from God. They therefore do not choose their identity for themselves, no matter how much they tinker with it, but receive it as an inalienable provision from Him. They do not name themselves; God names them.

On the one hand, every human being has been created in God's image with their bodies, minds, and all that they are. God Himself qualifies that by saying that they are made after His "likeness." They are like Him, yet not the same as Him. He does not create them as gods, but makes them to be Godlike creatures who receive their being from Him and are dependent on Him for their existence. Apart from Him, they are no different from the animals they resemble physically in so many ways, the animals that He created together with them (Genesis 1:24–25). But individually and collectively, personally and corporately, they are made to reflect Him in their humanity, just as each physical thing on earth shows the light of the sun that shines on it. They are made to reflect God's

10 For an analysis of what is meant by God's creation of humanity in His image, see John W. Kleinig, *Wonderfully Made: A Protestant Theology of the Body* (Lexham, 2021), 26–29.

glory, like a mirror that reflects my face without becoming a person like me. They have human bodies and minds, so that they can get to know Him and show what He is like as they communicate with Him and one another. What that means for them is left unexplained at this stage of human existence apart from God's blessing of them all and His call for them to work with Him in His care for the earth and its creatures (1:28).

On the other hand, God, most surprisingly, created them as either a man or a woman with their status as male or female. In that, they were not like God but, rather, like the higher animals with their sexuality. But unlike the animals, they were made by Him in His image with their male or female gender. Their right relationship with the opposite sex was meant to reflect their right relationship with God, and vice versa. Whether they were single or coupled, unmarried or married, they had the same common status as persons made in God's image and likeness. Yet as male and female, they were also made unique persons to show what God was like, each in their own way, in their relationship with the opposite sex and their own sex. So whether they knew it or not, their male or female bodies and personalities had the stamp of God on them, the call to life in communion with each other and with Him. They were made for personal life with God and each other.

As long as that was in order, Adam and Eve felt no shame, because their identity was secure. They were naked but not ashamed (Genesis 2:25).

The Onset of Shame

The story of Adam and Eve in Genesis 3 explores the nature of shame by considering its origin and connection with identity. It tells us seven things about shame: its original absence, its supernatural origin, its human cause, its connection with physical nakedness, its intermixture with guilt, the fallout from it, and God's help for dealing with it.

The first significant point is that shame was not an inherent part of Adam and Eve's humanity. God did not create shame when He made our first parents. It was not part of their original condition but a later modification of it. Nor did it arise from the need for adaptation to communal life and cooperation for survival in a hostile environment. Before Adam and Eve's fall from life with God, shame did not exist for them. They lived in the light of His glory as in the light of the sun. They were unselfconsciously naked and unashamed (Genesis 2:25).

Their subsequent shame did not originate from God, or even from their interaction with each other. It came from their seduction by a strange, supernatural creature, a mysterious, sweet-talking serpent who was more cunning and crafty than any other beast that God had created (3:1–5). As we later learn,[11] this hybrid creature, which was neither a true animal nor a real person, was the mouthpiece of the devil, the enemy of God and humanity, the evil spirit who wanted to supplant God and claim the world as his own domain. By listening to him rather than to God and by willingly

11 Isaiah 27:1; Revelation 12:3–4, 7–9.

complying with him, shame came on them with all its uncertainty and confusion, its self-accusation and self-condemnation. They traded their godly glory for sordid shame.

The actual, human cause of their shame was not just the infringement of God's prohibition against eating the fruit of the forbidden tree. It went much deeper than that and was far worse than that. Its cause was Eve's desire for spiritual autonomy, independence, and power, which Adam shared—the desire to be like God (3:4–5).[12] This is rather ironic and deluded because they were already like God, made as they were in God's image and likeness. But that was not good enough for them. It was not enough for them to be physical human beings who were to reflect God by their association and dependence on Him. They wanted to be divine in their own right, divine apart from God. They wanted to create their own identity; they wanted to be masters of their own lives with the power to choose what was best for them and others; they wanted to be omniscient and omnipotent (3:5). And immortal (3:3)! Behind that desire was their dissatisfaction with their physical, creaturely state, a desire that arose from their suspicion of God's goodwill for them and mistrust in Him. That, in turn, led to their disobedience and subsequent sense of shame, which was disclosed bodily in them by their nakedness. But unlike the guilt from the act of disobedience, their shame came from their hearts, their dissatisfaction with their actual God-given identity and their fanciful self-delusion. Their desire to be their own gods was the cause of their distrust and dissatisfaction, which produced evil

12 In Hebrew, the phrase "like God" is ambiguous. It could be understood as similar to God or the same as a god.

thoughts and desires, resulting in physical disobedience and the physical sense of shame. Their shame was the outcome, the manifestation of original sin for them, as it is for us. It shows us that there is something wrong with us—not just with some part of us or with something that we've done or left undone, but with the whole of us in body, soul, and spirit, because we fancy that we can live as our own gods. It is the index, the mark of our fallen state.

Even though the physical nakedness of Adam and Eve was associated with shame, it was not the cause of shame but a symptom of it. Originally, they were completely naked but not ashamed of it. They had no need to be ashamed of themselves because there was nothing wrong with them. They had nothing to hide. They realized that they were naked only after they disobeyed God. It was not the other way around. Their distrustful disobedience of God and His words opened their eyes to the shame of their nakedness. To their great dismay, they did not find any glory in their fancied identity (3:7, 10, 11). Instead, they saw what they were really like because they had fallen out with God and forfeited their God-given glory. Their nakedness exposed their shame. But it was not the reason for it. They were ashamed of what they had become and discovered how their desire for divine status had damaged their whole being and their relationship with God. So they were afraid to be seen by Him. They feared His disapproval and rejection. Their fear that God would see what they were really like in their hearts changed their attitude toward their naked bodies. They fancied that their physical sexuality was the only thing that was wrong with them. They imagined that if they covered their sexual organs and hid their barely covered bodies, they could hide themselves from God and so escape His disapproval.

But why were they so ashamed of their visible sexual organs when God had created them with these as either a male or a female person? Their sexual organs showed that they were not the same as God or even the same as each other. Their genitals showed them that they were not free, autonomous beings but creatures who were physically dependent on each other, just as their bodies showed that they depended on God for their existence. So instead of delighting in their complementary sexuality, as Adam had earlier done in Genesis 2:23, they were dissatisfied with it and ashamed of their gendered status with the limitations and demands that it placed on them. They were ashamed of how God had made them, and they wanted much more than what He had given them.

The shame of Adam and Eve was so closely associated and connected with their guilt that they did not distinguish between them. They confused their guilt with their shame, and vice versa, by their fixation on their nakedness. In reaction to the guilt of their rebellion against God, they were ashamed of their nakedness. That was why they covered themselves with fig leaves and hid from God. But the nakedness of their bodies was not the reason for their shame. They projected the shame from their rebellious hearts onto their genitals. It was as if the only thing that was wrong with them was their physical sexuality. To correct them from that delusion, God tried to get them to distinguish between their shame and guilt with His two leading questions to them, the first about why they felt so ashamed of their nakedness, and the second about whether they had disobeyed His commandment (3:11). But they either refused to answer Him or, perhaps more sadly, were so confused that they could not answer Him because they could not now distinguish between good and evil. Instead, they refused to face up to both their shame and their guilt by shifting the blame for what had happened. And that sets the pattern for us as their descendants. Like them, we confuse our guilt and shame and so need God's help to distinguish them.

The fallout from shame is far-reaching and complex. Since Adam was afraid of facing up to God and having to account for what had happened, he and Eve covered themselves with a lap cloth of fig leaves over their genitals.[13] Then, when they heard that God was coming to meet with them at the end of the day, they hid themselves from Him among the trees in the garden for fear of His disapproval and rejection of them. When God asked them what they had done, they avoided His question and evaded responsibility for their transgression. They justified themselves and excused their behavior to God—Adam by saying that he was afraid of God's scrutiny (3:10), and Eve by saying that the serpent had deceived her (3:13). Then, as their last resort, they tried to get rid of their shame by shifting the blame for what they had done and what had happened to them. Thus, Adam blamed Eve for his transgression as well as God Himself for giving her to him as his companion (3:12), and Eve blamed the serpent for it all (3:13). The fallout from shame unfolds with the sequence of consequences from the initial fear of God's rejection, to covering up to avoid disclosure, to hiding

13 The Hebrew word in Genesis 3:7 for this improvised piece of clothing refers to a kind of waist cloth that covers the loins with their sexual organs.

themselves to escape confrontation, to evasion of responsibility, to self-justification, and then, finally, to shifting the blame for their shame to another culprit.

Adam shamed Eve by shifting the blame onto her for what he himself had done and for his earlier failure to correct her and instruct her, which he could have and should have done, since he himself had been warned by God about what would happen if he ate the fruit of the forbidden tree (Genesis 2:17). We, too, intentionally or unintentionally, knowingly or unknowingly, shame those around us when we, like Adam, shift the blame in order to exonerate ourselves. We shame others when we do not honestly and willingly take the blame for what we have done, or, even, for what we have failed to do. We bring shame on others by failing to admit our wrongdoing and shortcomings and refusing to ask God for pardon and restoration. We wrongly justify ourselves at the expense of other people. But if we take the blame, we cover their shame and arrest its spread. We prevent it from damaging their relationship with us and undermining our relationship with them by our shameful self-righteousness.

This story of the origin of shame does not end with the fallout from it but with God's help in dealing with it and its effects. On the one hand, God, in His mercy, gives them a proper set of clothes made from the skin of animals that covers not just their genitals but also the whole of their all-too-vulnerable bodies. With these clothes, He protects them from physical abuse by their exposure and further shame from it. On the other hand, God, in His mercy, banishes them from the Garden of Eden so that they will not eat from the tree of life and live forever in their fallen state with its vexing guilt and perplexing shame. Thus He curtails the fallout from their rebellion for them and their descendants.

The story about the origin of shame sets the scene for the teaching on shame in the rest of the Bible. It is the first chapter of a long story about God's help in dealing with shame in life as it was lived east of Eden and His eventual deliverance of His people from it. It culminates in the creation of a new Adam and a new earth without guilt and shame.

A House with Six Pillars

Adam and Eve could not blame anyone except themselves for their shameful condition after their rebellion against God. Their shame came from their failure to listen to God, trust in Him, and live as people created in His image. They did not just fail to do what God wanted them to do but also to be as God had created them to be. They desired to be divine in their own right, free from God to forge their own self-chosen selves apart from Him. Their shame came from their failure to be like Him.

But things changed for their descendants who, unlike them, were born into a disordered world that was riddled with unrighteousness and injustice. Thus for us, like them, the worst shame that we now experience does not, in practice, come from our loss of innocence but from our experience of injustice from those in power. We are ashamed when people who have some power over us promote themselves at our expense by abusing and oppressing us. But what is bad is made worse when those who are called to exercise justice—such as parents and teachers, bosses and politicians, police and judges—side with those who oppress us and use the positions of power to excuse themselves for their wrongdoing.

The whole of the Old Testament is the story of God's exercise of justice to protect people from shame and to free them from the scourge of injustice. It tells of His work as the Judge of all people who condemns those who are wicked and vindicates those who are righteous. That divine strategy is summed up quite simply by God Himself in Psalm 75:2–5, where He gives this assurance and warning:

> [2]At the set time that I appoint
> I will judge with equity.
> [3]When the earth totters, and all its inhabitants,
> it is I who keep steady its pillars.
> [4]I say to the boastful, "Do not boast,"
> and to the wicked, "Do not lift up your horn;
> [5]do not lift up your horn on high,
> or speak with a haughty neck."

Then, in verse 10, He sums up His purpose with this decree:

> [10]All the horns of the wicked I will cut off,
> but the horns of the righteous shall be lifted up.[14]

14 The speaker in this verse is unidentified. It is either the psalmist, as in verse 9, or God, as in verses 2–5. If it is the psalmist, he disempowers the wicked and empowers the righteous by his song of thanksgiving for God's just acts of judgment.

In verses 6–8, the psalmist explains that before God does that, He disables the wicked, like people who have been forced to drink a drug that confuses and paralyzes them.

In this statement about the purpose of His judgment, God uses two vivid metaphors. First, He compares the earth to a well-built house for its inhabitants that is held up by a set of strong stone pillars.[15] Second, He compares their leaders to large bulls with powerful horns that should be used to protect the members of their household from attack by another powerful ruler rather than misused to abuse them.

God executes justice in two ways. On the one hand, He intervenes to steady the pillars of the house that He has established as a safe place for His people on earth. When its pillars are shaken so severely by an attack on them, like a house by an earthquake, that both the earth and its inhabitants are about to totter, He secures the house in order to keep its residents safe from damage and destruction. On the other hand, when the leaders whom He has appointed to administer justice together with Him attack the pillars of the house by their abuse of power, He first warns them of His judgment on them and then, if they do not heed His warning, He disempowers and demotes them. He puts them down from the position of honor and power and lifts up others to replace them (Psalm 75:6–7).

Well, what are the pillars of the earth, and how do they protect its residents from shame? They are the pillars of institutions that

15 See the use of the same picture in 1 Samuel 2:8; Job 38:4. The pillars of the earth are also envisaged as its foundations in Psalms 11:3 and 82:5.

God established in the world for human life on earth, institutions that uphold natural and moral order for human communities. They do not create our inherent, God-given identity but confirm it in human terms. They affirm the honor that is conferred on everybody and protect the social status that follows from its endowment. So, for example, the domestic status of parents comes from their call to represent God to their children, and the sexual status of married people comes from God's creation of them as men or women and His union of them in marriage.

There are six basic pillars of a just, safe social order. They are presupposed and protected by the second table of the Ten Commandments, which until recently were the foundation for our legal order. They were given to the Israelites by God Himself at Mount Sinai as part of His covenant with them. Here they are as they are written in Exodus 20:12–17:

> 12 Honor your father and your mother, that your days may be long in the land that the LORD your God is giving you.
>
> 13 You shall not murder.
>
> 14 You shall not commit adultery.
>
> 15 You shall not steal.
>
> 16 You shall not bear false witness against your neighbor.
>
> 17 You shall not covet your neighbor's house; you shall not covet your neighbor's wife, or his male servant, or his female servant, or his ox, or his donkey, or anything that is your neighbor's.

The first pillar of a just social order is the right of the extended family as an institution with the relationship between parents and children at its heart. Through the parents, God provides life and nurture, protection and discipline to the children. The children also receive their identity from God, with its sense of worth and self-esteem through their parents. Without the acceptance and approval of their parents, the children's sense of self is unstable and insecure. They are readily shamed by real or imagined slights and easily damaged by criticism and the lack of affirmation. But the love and affection, the acceptance and approval of both their father and mother give children a good social foundation for their sense of self and their true worth. That works properly and most effectively when children respect and honor their parents, no matter how fallible and imperfect they may be. From the honor that they show to their parents, they learn to become good parents themselves. But if they dishonor their parents, they bring shame on themselves and their whole family. The family is therefore the first line of defense against shame, just as domestic abuse is a prime cause of shame.

The second pillar of a just social order is the right to life that is expressed by the prohibition of murder and protected by the courts of law. It has to do with the importance of the human body and its place in human life. We are all embodied persons, and our true sense of self—our real identity—is tied up with our bodies, so much so that when we think of ourselves, we usually first think of our bodies. The prohibition of murder protects our bodies from all other kinds of physical violence and abuse that shame us so severely. Since we were made in God's image with our bodies and receive life from Him, murder is an attack on Him (Genesis 9:6). The right to life in the body is therefore the second line of defense against shame, just as physical abuse is a common cause of shame.

The third pillar of a safe social order is the right of marriage, with its exclusive, permanent sexual union between a man and a woman. Its stability and integrity are protected by the prohibition of adultery, because adultery damages both the husband and wife as well as their children and grandchildren. Adultery and all kinds of sexual abuse damage sexuality because they affect who we are, our God-given identity as a man or a woman, male or female. The result is sexual confusion and disorder. And acute shame! The sexual unfaithfulness of one spouse dishonors the other spouse. That's why Luther, in his catechetical explanation of this commandment, urges both husband and wife to honor each other. The faithfulness of both in their marriage provides the context for the enjoyment of sexual intercourse without embarrassment and shame. The institution of marriage is therefore the third line of defense against shame, just as sexual abuse is a common cause of shame.

The fourth pillar of a safe social order is the right of property, which is protected by the prohibition of theft and all other kinds of economic exploitation. The property of a family ensures and secures the life of its members. For better or worse, their personal status in society, their sense of worth and importance, depends on their economic status. It also determines their occupation and participation in the life of their community and their identity. Thus, when I consider myself, I think of my vocation and the things that belong to me. They are part of who I am. You can see this most clearly in the bitter wrangling of family members over the inheritance that they receive from their parents, as if that were the final proof of their true status and worth in the family. Theft does not just deprive me of my property. It shames me. It affects me personally and breaks down the trust that provides security for me in my community. So the right of property is the fourth line of defense against shame, just as economic abuse is another common course of shame.

The fifth pillar of a safe social order is the right to a good reputation, with its prohibition of false witness in a court of law and the court of public opinion. It refers to all kinds of misrepresentation, defamation, and slander that aim to destroy someone's social status and honor. This is by far the most common cause of shame in any community. It does such great damage because it is a direct attack on a person's proper name and personal identity, the person's sense of self and sense of worth. So the right to a good reputation is the fifth line of defense against shame, just as verbal abuse is a very common cause of shame.

The sixth pillar of a safe social order is the right to a livelihood, with the institution of a household as an economic unit in society. In the ancient world, the Greek word for housekeeping, *economy*, was used for the management of the assets of a household as well as the assets of a whole city or a nation. The prohibition of covetousness and greed protected the livelihood of each extended family, with all its personal and material assets, its means of production as its life-support system. This prohibition presupposed the role of the wife as the steward of the whole household. She was its housekeeper. She was assisted by the servants and animals that belonged to the family. The house was the center of the family farm, which depended on her management as well as the work of male and female servants, with the help of oxen and donkeys for its survival and productivity. So the desire for these assets and any schemes to deprive that family of them threatened the survival of the household. It could lead to its impoverishment and dispossession and the breakdown of the family. To put it in modern terms, the prohibition of covetousness guards against bankruptcy by the underhanded or illegal takeover of a family business. So the right to its livelihood is the sixth line of defense against shame, just as economic abuse is a common cause of shame.

The Rule of Law

By His covenant with the Israelites at Mount Sinai, God established the rule of Law, His Law for them and all people, His Law by which He revealed Himself to them as their Lawgiver and supreme Judge (Exodus 20:1–17; Deuteronomy 5:1–21). As their Lawgiver and Judge, God the Creator maintains the six main social pillars by which He protects people from shame. When these pillars are shaken by wrongdoing, He steadies them by calling the wrongdoers to account. He does not act in an arbitrary way but according to His own standards as set out in the Ten Commandments. He applies His Law to His people and enacts it through those He appoints to administer His justice, such as parents or magistrates. He judges people with equity by vindicating those who have experienced abuse and injustice and by punishing the wrongdoers. He puts the wicked to shame and protects the righteous from shame.

God's Law is the standard by which people can distinguish the warranted shame and dishonor of an evildoer, such as a rapist, from the unwarranted shame and dishonor of a victim, such as a woman who has been raped. Thus the rule of God's Law distinguishes guilt from shame. It frees the victims of abuse from unjustified guilt and assures them that they do not need to be ashamed of what has happened to them. It is His guiding light for them in an unjust world.[16] It encourages them to appeal to God in prayer to vindicate them[17] and to shame those who have shamed them.[18]

Yet all these measures are an exercise in damage control. Through His exercise of justice and the moral order that it upholds, God keeps a check on shame, so that it does not get out of hand and lead to the abuse of power by the compulsion to seek revenge. But by itself, the rule of Law and its maintenance of a just social order cannot undo the deep-seated cause of shame by the human fall into sin. It can modify human behavior, but it cannot change the corrupt human heart, with its mistaken quest for its own self-chosen identity apart from God. That requires a much more radical solution: the creation of a new heart in God's image and likeness.[19]

16 See the repeated recourse to God's commands and promise for protection and deliverance from shame in Psalm 119:6, 31, 46, 80, 116.

17 See Psalm 35:24–26.

18 See Psalms 6:10; 35:1–4, 24–26; 40:13–14; 70:1–3; 86:16–17.

19 See the prophecy of God's atonement for sin in Ezekiel 16:63 and His promise of cleansing and a heart transplant for His people in Ezekiel 36:24–32.

Questions for Reflection and Discussion

1. Is there anything in this chapter that you would like to discuss?

2. In what ways is our sense of shame connected with our sense of self, that is, our identity?

3. How is our identity dependent on our relationship with God and the people close to us?

4. Why has shame staged a sudden comeback in our society? How has this happened?

5. How does the story of the fall in Genesis 3 help you to understand your experience of shame?

6. What did God do after the fall to protect all people from injustice and the chronic shame that it produces?

CHAPTER THREE

Waiting for Vindication

How long, O Lord, will You look on? Rescue me [my soul] from their destruction, my precious life from the lions!

(Psalm 35:17)

How long? That is the heartfelt cry of disadvantaged people around the world. That was the lament of a man I got to know recently, a homeless man we have helped to get back on his feet. When he heard that I was writing a book on shame, he told me that he could tell me a lot about that from his own experience. After his wife died from cancer, the bottom fell out of his life. He spiraled into severe depression. He lost everything he had and ended up living on the streets in our city. The shame of public vagrancy and dependence on public welfare was made worse after another vagrant person violently assaulted him. In desperation, he took refuge in the porch of our church hall. That's where I found him one Sunday morning before church. Since then, my wife and I have been helping him in his rehabilitation and the recovery of his personal dignity and worth. We helped him find a safe place to live; first, for a while, in our house, and then in a furnished shed in our backyard. Through all of that, he has regained a sense of personal safety with acceptance by our congregation, faith in Jesus, and protection by the police.

How long? That cry echoes down through the ages from people who have been shamed by injustice while longing for deliverance. It is repeated by God's people in the Old Testament as they wait for Him to deliver and vindicate them. All too often, it seems as if God is indifferent to their plight. He seems to be a distant spectator who sees how people suffer but does little or nothing to help them. In their impatience, they beg Him not to delay any longer. Why does He not step in and fix things up once and for all time? Why are the wicked not held to account? Why does God not punish them for their wickedness? Where can they find a place of safety from injustice?

Even though we may think God is slow to judge, He does punish the wicked by visiting the consequences of their iniquity on them (Exodus 34:7). He brings the evil of evildoers back on them. But His punishment of evildoers, whether in Israel or the nations, is a stopgap, provisional measure before His final day of judgment. By itself, punishment does not deal with the fallout from injustice unless it is coupled with God's pardon for the repentant wrongdoer and the vindication of the victim. That is God's promise to His people through the prophets who foretell His eventual judgment on all evildoing and final vindication of those who hope in Him for their salvation (Isaiah 45:17). God Himself promises: "Those who wait for Me shall not be put to shame" (49:23).

Yet that message is itself rather puzzling because it is so paradoxical. Yes, God's people will be vindicated, but only after being shamed with defeat by their enemies and exiled from their land for their evildoing (Zephaniah 3:14–20). Yes, the nations that had oppressed them will be punished for their wickedness, but only to induce them to turn to the Lord in repentance and seek vindication from Him together with His people (Isaiah 45:22–25). Yes, God will fight for His people and defeat their greatest foe, who was also the common enemy of all people on earth (25:6–8). Yes, God will appoint a righteous king as His agent, His servant to free all people from oppression, not by the exercise of punitive power but by His unjust death as a sacrifice for their transgressions (50:4–9; 52:13–53:12). Yes, God will provide a place of refuge from shame in the rebuilt city of Jerusalem, but only for all those who put their trust in Him rather than in their own social and political power (28:16).

A Divine Place of Refuge

When the people of Judah and the citizens of Jerusalem were threatened by the powerful Assyrian army, they tried to protect themselves from defeat and destruction in two ways. On the one hand, led by their king, Hezekiah, they rearmed their troops and rebuilt the walls of Jerusalem for the imminent siege and attack (2 Chronicles 32:1–5). On the other hand, as is mentioned in Isaiah 28:14–18 and 30:1–5, they also forged a treaty with the Egyptians, a treaty that they imagined would provide a refuge for them from the Assyrian army (30:1–2). This futile alliance with that pagan superpower was backed by the threat of death for its infringement by Seth, the Egyptian god of the underworld and death (28:15, 18). It was then that God made this promise to His people in Isaiah 28:16–17:[20]

20 This is my own composite translation.

> 16 Behold, I am laying in Zion a foundation stone,[21]
> a tested stone,[22]
> a precious[23] cornerstone,
> a sure foundation:[24]
> "Whoever believes will not be put to shame."[25]
> 17 And I will make justice the measuring line
> and righteousness the plumb line;[26]
> and hail will sweep away the refuge of lies,
> and waters will overwhelm the shelter.

In face of the threat from the powerful Assyrian army, the citizens of Jerusalem relied on the fortifications of the city and their alliance with the Egyptians for their security and safety. This was their refuge, their secure stronghold against the Assyrian army. But in reality, this refuge was little more than a flimsy hut that would be swept away by a flood from a severe thunderstorm. It would be washed away because it had been built on nothing more than the sinking sand of unbelief and pride, self-delusion and lies. God Himself threatens to sweep this insecure refuge away and replace it with a new city of refuge, a supernatural fortress that He Himself will set on a new foundation stone.[27] God promises to build a

---

21 This recalls the declaration in Isaiah 14:32 of God's foundation of Zion as a place of refuge for His afflicted people.

22 Literally, "a stone of testing." This is the term for a stone that has been tested to ensure its specific shape so that it can be used for the exact alignment of all other stones that are placed next to it and upon it.

23 See Isaiah 54:11–12.

24 Oddly, the foundation of the city is this unexplained promise, which does not tell who is addressed, who or what they are to believe, and how they will be kept free from shame. The mention of faith recalls God's promise to King Ahaz in Isaiah 7:9.

25 For this verb, I follow the Greek translation of the Old Testament, which is quoted in Romans 9:33; 10:11; 1 Peter 2:6.

26 For the combination of justice and righteousness, see Isaiah 1:27; 5:7, 16; 9:7; 32:1, 16; 33:5; 56:1; 59:9, 14–17. Here God's justice has to do with His judgment on His people, and righteousness refers to His subsequent vindication of them.

27 In 2:4–6 of his first letter, Peter teaches that Jesus is the foundation for a new temple, which, as John shows in Revelation 21:22–27, will be the heavenly city that God will build on earth.

strong city for them on a completely reliable, trustworthy foundation stone, a precisely cut and exactly measured precious cornerstone, so that all the other stones can rest on it and be aligned with it. That stone is a new King, a Second David, whom God will use to build this city. The city will rest on this King by its faith in Him. It will be established by God's administration of justice and righteousness through this King. The city and its citizens will depend on this future King for their safety and will trust in Him for their deliverance from shame. This city will provide a sanctuary from shame for those who reside in it.[28] Neither the city nor its citizens will ever be shaken, as long as they rest on that secure foundation.[29]

From Shame to Praise

The history of Jerusalem should have been a story of trust in God's presence with them in His temple and the reliance on His justice and righteousness for protection from shame. Instead, it was, by and large, the story of shameless rebellion against God and the abuse of power with personal and institutionalized injustice (Isaiah 1:21–23; Zephaniah 3:1–5). As God had warned, He dealt justly with Jerusalem by allowing the Babylonians to sack it and deport its citizens into exile in order to purge it and restore its penitent survivors (Isaiah 1:24–31; Zephaniah 3:9–13).

God promises the citizens of Jerusalem that after their restoration they will never again be put to shame for their rebellion against God (Zephaniah 3:11–13). Then, in 3:14–20, the prophet

28 See all God's later promises about the new, heavenly city of Jerusalem in Isaiah 35; 49:14–26; 51:17–52:2; 54; 60; 62:1–9; 65:17–25; 66:7–13.

29 See Matthew 16:18; Acts 4:11–12; 1 Corinthians 3:11; Ephesians 2:19–22.

Zephaniah explains what will happen after the restoration of Jerusalem:

> *14*Sing aloud, O daughter Zion;[30]
>   shout, O Israel!
> Rejoice and exult with all your heart,
>   O daughter Jerusalem!
> *15*The LORD has taken away the judgments against you;[31]
>   he has turned away your enemies.
> The king of Israel, the LORD, is in your midst;
>   you shall fear disaster no more.
> *16*On that day[32] it shall be said to Jerusalem:
> "Do not fear, O Zion;
>   do not let your hands grow weak.
> *17*The LORD, your God, is in your midst,
>   a warrior who gives victory;
> he will rejoice over you with gladness;
>   he will renew you in his love;
> he will exult over you with loud singing
> *18* as on a day of festival."
> I will remove disaster from you,
>   so that you will not bear reproach[33] for it.

---

30 Zion was originally the name for the center of Jerusalem, its acropolis on a hill, its stronghold that combined the holy temple, the royal palace, and the military headquarters.

31 The picture here seems to be God's amnesty for Jerusalem, which canceled His charges against her and the penalty for her rebellion against Him.

32 This is the stock formula for God's final day of judgment and salvation, the day when He will punish the wicked and vindicate the righteous. Here, Zephaniah shows how the return of God's people from exile in Babylon will foreshadow that eventual day of salvation.

33 "Reproach" is the term for abusive speech that intends to blame and shame the person that it attacks. It is a kind of character assassination, with words as the weapons of choice. It covers the full range of verbal abuse and disparagement, from criticism and censure to false accusation and condemnation, from slander to scorn and mockery, from insulting remarks to denunciation. It also refers to the consequent emotional sense of disrespect and disgrace that makes the belittled person feel despised and rejected, discredited and worthless. And it describes the public disgrace that comes from all these kinds of

[19]I will deal with all your oppressors at that time.
And I will save the lame[34]
and gather the outcast,
and I will change their shame into praise
and renown in all the earth.
[20]At that time I will bring you home,
at the time when I gather you;
for I will make you renowned and praised
among all the peoples of the earth,[35]
when I restore your fortunes
before your eyes, says the LORD. (NRSVue)

Shame destroys joy and arouses fear. Delivery from shame dispels fearful sadness and awakens fearless joy.

On the future day of the Lord—His final day of retribution and vindication—God Himself will change the fearful, disabling, discouraging shame of Zion into three kinds of praise: her song of praise to God for deliverance from her enemies, His song of joy for her as His beloved Bride, and the praise of her by the nations for her transformation.

First, in Zephaniah 3:14–15, there is a call to Zion to praise God with all her heart because she will no longer have any reason to fear disaster. She will have nothing to fear because God Himself will pardon her, free her from the threat of attack by her enemies, and reside with her as her King. This is followed in 3:16–18a by a warm word of encouragement that removes her fear of disaster and

derisive remarks that aim to undermine the reputation and social status of a rival.

34 See also Isaiah 35:6 and Micah 4:6–7a.

35 This recalls God's promise in Deuteronomy 26:19.

enables her to act confidently. Her fearless confidence will depend on God's presence with her as a champion warrior and her loving husband. As her powerful bodyguard, He will protect her and keep her safe; as her loving husband, He will rejoice over her with His song of love for her and delight in His renewed union with her. Then in 3:18b–20, we have God's own promise to transform her public disgrace into international praise. He will free her from the burden of blame for her defeat and destruction by delivering her exiled citizens from oppression by her enemies, bringing them back home to her and making her the most famous city on earth. Then all the nations will recognize, honor, and praise her as the city of God. Like Zion, all her citizens will then also be pardoned and protected, victorious and loved, blameless and praiseworthy.

A Marriage Restored

In a tribal society, such as ancient Israel, the male head of an extended family was its redeemer. That was the term for the man who had the duty to care for the family as a community and all its members as important parts of it. So when a crime was committed against someone in the family, the redeemer brought the offender into the local court of law to gain justice for the victim and avenge the crime. If his kinsfolk were falsely accused of a crime, he served as an advocate for them in a trial. If anyone in the family was enslaved as a debtor or a prisoner of war, he paid the ransom for the debtor's release. If one of the married men in his family died without fathering a male heir, he arranged to enter a de facto relationship with the man's widow to raise a male heir for her and retain the land that belonged to her former husband. It was therefore the duty of a redeemer to protect his family from shameful injustice and oppression. He defended the honor of the family.

In Isaiah 54:1–9, God calls Zion His estranged wife and Himself both her "husband" and "Redeemer." She had much to be ashamed of in her relationship with Him. Their relationship had begun in shame with her status as a slave in Egypt before He redeemed her from slavery and married her at Sinai; it culminated in the shame of her enslavement as a prisoner of war in Babylon for her faithlessness. Yet despite that, He assures her that He will redeem her and end her acute shame. This is what He says to her in 54:4–8:

> 4"Fear not, for you will not be ashamed;
> be not confounded, for you will not be disgraced;
> for you will forget the shame of your youth,[36]
> and the reproach[37] of your widowhood you will
> remember no more.
> 5For your Maker is your husband,
> the LORD of hosts is His name;
> and the Holy One of Israel is your Redeemer,
> the God of the whole earth He is called.
> 6For the LORD has call you
> like a wife deserted and grieved in spirit,
> like a wife of youth when she is cast off,
> says your God.
> 7For a brief moment I deserted you,

36 See Jeremiah 3:24–25; 31:19.
37 Or "disgrace." See footnote 33.

but with great compassion I will gather you.
[8]In overflowing anger for a moment
I hid My face from you,
but with everlasting love I will have compassion on you,"
says the Lord, your Redeemer.

Even though God had abandoned Zion for her faithlessness by banishing her from His presence, He promises to have compassion on her and call her back to Himself. Just as He had covered the shame of her youth when she was a slave in Egypt by His marriage to her, so He assures her that He will make her forget the disgrace of her de facto widowhood by His renewed commitment to her. She therefore has no reason to fear that she will ever again be shamed. She will never again be put to shame, because she has such a kind, compassionate husband. His new covenant with her and His steadfast love for her will keep her safe and give her peace (54:9–10). Since He will vindicate and defend her, she will be able to refute every tongue that will rise in judgment against her (54:17).

The Feast for Death's Defeat

In the ancient world, the greatest shame for any nation and its king was incurred by their defeat in battle. That brought shame on the nation's gods as well, because they had proved to be too weak and powerless and unconcerned to save their people from destruction. By contrast, the greatest honor, the greatest glory, was gained by a king with a decisive victory over a national enemy. His victory was celebrated with a great feast of rejoicing that he hosted in his palace for his soldiers and courtiers.

Like the other nations, the Israelites also celebrated victories over their enemies with feasting and rejoicing. But they had a different focus, because their God was not one of many would-be national gods. He was the Lord of hosts, the commander in chief of all earthly and heavenly armies. He commanded the armies of the nations as well as the armies of Israel. Since He was the God of Israel, He defended His people against unjust attacks and gave them the victory over their enemies. His people then quite rightly celebrated the victory with a service of thanksgiving and a feast hosted by Him at His temple in Jerusalem.[38]

The prophet Isaiah predicts an amazing feast to celebrate God's defeat of Israel's last, worst enemy, a terrible tyrant who was not just their enemy but also the enemy of all people and all nations. In 25:6–9, he tells how God, the Lord of hosts, will host a great feast to celebrate the death of death:

> 6On this mountain[39] the LORD of hosts will make for all peoples
> a feast of rich food, a feast of well-aged wine,
> of rich food filled with marrow, of aged wine well refined.
> 7And He will swallow up on this mountain
> the covering that is cast over all peoples,
> the veil[40] that is spread over all nations.
> 8 He will swallow up death forever;[41]

38 For a psalm of thanksgiving for a victory, see Psalm 118.

39 The mountain is Mount Zion, the site of God's holy temple and His city, the future place of worship for all nations (Isaiah 2:2–4).

40 While this is often taken as the veil that covered the faces of people who mourned the loss of their loved ones, its association with the shrouds of those who were buried shows that it most likely refers to the grave cloths that covered the faces of corpses when interred or buried.

41 Or else "in victory."

and the Lord GOD will wipe away the tears from all faces,
and the reproach[42] of His people He will take away from all the earth,
for the LORD has spoken.
9It will be said on that day,[43]
"Behold, this is our God; we have waited for Him, that He might save us.[44]
This is the LORD; we have waited for Him;
let us be glad and rejoice in His salvation."[45]

Note the international scope of this meal. It will be provided for *all peoples* (25:6) because God will destroy the shrouds and face coverings of *all peoples* (25:7) from *all nations*, wipe away tears from *all faces*, and remove the disgrace of His people from *all the earth* (25:8).

Isaiah's prophecy of a feast to celebrate the death of death is full of surprises. First, God Himself will host this meal on Mount Zion with the best food and the finest wine. Second, the guests will not just be the people of Israel but will also include people from all nations, even those who were once its enemies. Third, the enemy that will be defeated is death itself. Its defeat is described in graphic terms. Both Israel and its neighbors imagined death as a monster with a large mouth and huge stomach because it had such an insatiable appetite and swallowed up all living creatures on earth. But that will be reversed. The living God will gobble up this terrible gobbler. He will not just conquer death but also destroy it forever,

42 See footnote 33.
43 See footnote 32.
44 Or "give us the victory."
45 Or "victory."

so that it can no longer destroy any life on earth. By swallowing death, God will also swallow the grave cloths of those who had died and been buried, so that they can see and be seen alive once again. Fourth—most significant for this discussion on shame—God Himself will wipe away the tears from all the faces of all the people by removing the reproach and disgrace of His people from all the earth. That disgrace, that cause of shame and blame, is the sentence of death that has haunted every human being on earth, and even God's own people, since Adam and Eve ate the fruit from the tree of death, the tree of the knowledge of good and evil. On the day of salvation, all people who have waited for God's victory over death will acknowledge Him as their God and celebrate the international feast for His victory over death with gladness and rejoicing.

In 1 Corinthians 15:53–54 and 2 Corinthians 5:4, Paul teaches that all those who trust in Jesus will be raised bodily from death to celebrate that victory with thanksgiving. They will give thanks that Jesus has ended the disgrace of sin with its penalty of eternal death by His death and resurrection. They will give thanks to God, who gave them the victory through their Lord Jesus Christ (1 Corinthians 15:57).

Shamed but Not Disgraced

Consider God's dilemma. How can He punish the sins of all people and also vindicate the victims of sin? How can He remove the burden of guilt and shame from those who turn to Him for deliverance?

The answer to that vital question is given by God through Isaiah in a series of prophecies about His commission of a new king as His righteous servant and royal deputy.[46] This divine agent will be someone like Moses, Aaron, and David but greater than them, because they all failed to fulfill God's entire purpose for the world and its inhabitants. He will be called the Messiah, the Christ, because God Himself will anoint Him with His Holy Spirit to administer His righteousness and justice (Isaiah 11:1–9; 61:1–3). Even though He will be despised and abhorred by the people He came to save (49:7), He will bring God's salvation to the ends of the earth (42:6–7; 49:6). Surprisingly, He will accomplish His mission by what He suffers rather than by what He does. Shamed, He will free people from their guilt and shame.

This is how God's Suffering Servant describes what happens to Him in Isaiah 50:4–9:

> 4The Lord God has given Me
>   the tongue of those who are taught,
> that I may know how to sustain with a word
>   him who is weary.[47]
> Morning by morning He awakens,
>   He awakens My ear
>   to hear as those who are taught.
> 5The Lord God has opened My ear,
>   and I was not rebellious;
>   I turned not backward.

46 See the four so-called Servant Songs in Isaiah 42:1–9; 49:1–13; 50:4–11; 52:13–53:12.

47 See Isaiah 40:27–31.

[6]I gave My back to those who strike,
and My cheeks to those who pull out the beard.
I hid not My face
from disgrace and spitting.

[7]But the Lord God helps Me;
therefore I have not been disgraced;
therefore I have set My face like flint,
and I know that I shall not be put to shame.
[8]He who vindicates Me is near.
Who will contend with Me?
Let us stand up together.
Who is My adversary?
Let him come near to Me.
[9]Behold, the Lord God helps Me;
who will declare Me guilty?
Behold, all of them will wear out like a garment;
the moth will eat them up.

In this eloquent poem, God's Servant describes how God helps Him in three different situations. He helps Him as a student who is taught by God as He listens daily to His voice, so that He could comfort others with the word that He has heard. He helps Him as a patient, an unshaken victim of physical abuse that was meant to shame Him. He helps Him as an innocent person on trial in a court of law. With ears that are open to God's instruction and direction, He willingly submits to the full range of physical abuse by His opponents that was designed to shame Him and incite Him to defy God's will for Him as a student and teacher of God's Word.

In obedience to God, He offers His back to be beaten, His cheeks to have His beard pulled, and His face to be spit upon and mocked as gestures of utter contempt for Him. But despite these malicious attacks on Him, He sets His face as hard as flint and refuses to let them break Him. He bears the shame of their abuse because He knows that He has God's backing. He knows that no matter what is done to disgrace Him, He will not be put to shame. No one will ever be able to charge Him with any offense, nor will anyone ever be able to condemn Him, because God is His Advocate and Judge. He is certain that God will vindicate Him. By what He suffered and endured, He was taught by God what to say and how to sustain His weary disciples who waited for God to vindicate them. He will sustain them with the same words that sustained Him in His suffering.

The reason for His willing acceptance of shame is given later in Isaiah 52:13–53:12. There we discover that God's Servant will not just submit to physical and verbal abuse to equip Him to sustain people who were burdened with guilt and shame, but He will also be put to death as a vicarious sacrifice (53:4–5, 10, 12b). In fact, God will lay on Him the iniquity of all people (53:6). He will bear their pain and suffering (53:4); He will bear the guilt of human sin and the burden of human transgression (53:11). He will pour out His soul in death and be raised to life to vindicate many people (53:10–11); He will cleanse them from the stain of guilt and shame with His blood (52:13–15a). In 53:11–12, God Himself explains what His Servant will accomplish by His sacrificial death:

> [11]Out of the anguish of His soul He shall see and be satisfied;
> by His knowledge shall the righteous one, My servant,

make many to be accounted righteous,
and He shall bear[48] their iniquities. . . .

*12*Yet He bore the sin of many,[49]
and makes intercession for the transgressors.

The death of God's Servant will be followed by His resurrection. Since He has taken the sin of all people on His shoulders and interceded for all transgressors,[50] He will justify them by pardoning the wrongdoers and vindicating those who had been wronged.

Waiting for Vindication

Well, what does the Old Testament tell us about God's help for people who have shamed themselves by their evildoing and been shamed by the evil that has been done to them? That topic crops up in many places across the whole of it. But it is mentioned from so many different points of view and in so many different contexts that it is hard to see how it all fits together. It's a bit like a jigsaw puzzle with many pieces or the loose pages of a book without some pages and no last chapter. But when read in the light of the story of Jesus, it all comes together and makes good sense.

When we look back on the story of shame in the Old Testament from its fulfillment by Jesus as the Messiah, its teaching on shame culminates in what God Himself says in Isaiah 45:22–25:

48 This Hebrew verb, *sābal,* refers to carrying a load on the back. The load is God's penalty for sin. The result of Jesus carrying that load is God's pardon of sinners and His release of them from its effects.

49 Here, as in Isaiah 52:14, 15; 53:11, "many" is an inclusive Hebrew idiom for all people, the total sum of humankind, rather than a few people or no people. See also Matthew 20:28; Mark 10:45; Romans 5:15; Hebrews 9:28. Likewise, "sin" is an inclusive term for what was done by wrongdoers as well as what was done to those whom they had wronged.

50 See Luke 23:24.

22 Turn to Me and be saved, all you ends of the earth!
For I am God, and there is no other.
23 By Myself[51] I have sworn,
from My mouth has gone out in righteousness
a word that shall not return:[52]
"To Me every knee will bow;
every tongue shall swear allegiance."

24 Only in the LORD, it shall be said of Me,
are righteousness and strength;
to Him shall come and be ashamed
all who were incensed against Him.
25 In the LORD all the offspring of Israel
shall be justified[53] and shall glory.

Here God invites people from all the earth to turn to Him as their God to receive salvation. He promises to deliver them from injustice and sin and death. He makes that promise to all people on earth. But only those who turn to Him and acknowledge Him as the one true God will be saved. He backs up that invitation to all people with an oath and a decree. He swears by Himself that eventually all people will have to submit to Him and admit that He is the only source of righteousness and strength, righteousness as justification and vindication, and strength as the power to overcome evil and rely on Him for help. Then those who raged against Him will be ashamed of their rejection and be able to come to Him

51 Usually people swear an oath by invoking God to punish them if they break it. Here God backs up His oath by offering Himself as a guarantee for its fulfillment. See also Genesis 22:16; Jeremiah 22:5; 49:13; 51:14; Amos 6:8.

52 Compare this with God's decree in Isaiah 55:11.

53 Or "vindicated."

as their God, while all the faithful remnant of Israel will come to Him to be justified and vindicated by Him. Then they will glory in Him rather than themselves. They will have everlasting salvation and will never again be put to shame (Isaiah 45:17).

According to Paul's teaching in Romans 14:10–11 and Philippians 2:10, the speaker in Isaiah 45:22–25 is the risen Lord Jesus. He is the Lord of both Jews and Gentiles. By His Word, He brings them together as the new people of God. By His Word, He frees wrongdoers from guilt by justifying the wrongdoers who relied on Him for pardon from sin and vindicating the victims of wrongdoing who relied on Him for deliverance from shame.

Questions for Reflection and Discussion

1. Is there anything in this chapter that you would like to discuss?

2. Have you, like God's people in the Old Testament, ever been upset because God has not punished those who have abused you?

3. Why does God hold back from passing His final judgment on evildoers and vindicating people who have been unjustly shamed?

4. Discuss the relevance of God's promises to free His people from shame in the following ways:

   - By establishing the new, holy city of Jerusalem by a Second David as His place of refuge for them
   - By His presence with His people in Zion to turn their sorrow into joy and their shame into praise

- By our reunion with God, through Jesus, which is like the reunion of a faithless wife with her faithful husband
- By His victory over death and His feast to celebrate it with them
- By sending the Messiah to bear their shame and free them from it through His suffering, death, and resurrection

5. Which of these promises means the most to you?

6. In what ways are we as Christians still waiting to be vindicated?

CHAPTER FOUR

Crying Out for Help

Those who look to Him are radiant,
and their faces shall never be ashamed.

(Psalm 34:5)

Where can those who have been unjustly shamed find help for themselves, so that they are not undone by their shame?

They can take matters into their own hands by trying to shame those who have shamed them. But that only adds guilt to their sense of shame and does not provide the expected emotional relief from it. They can try to forget the shame by repressing it. But that merely imprints it deeply on them, so that it secretly haunts them and drives them to compensate for it by angling for approval. They can deny shame's emotional effect by pretending that it does not matter. But that desensitizes them in themselves and their relationship with others. So, despite their best efforts, they are usually stuck with shame and its impact on them.

In their distress, they would like to unburden themselves to someone who would at least hear them out and sympathize with them. But to do that, they need to overcome their sense of embarrassment and their fear of rejection. After all, no one likes a whinger,[54] let alone an angry whinger! If they eventually break their silence and pour out their hearts to an attentive hearer, an emotionally charged complaint bursts out—an unfocused, wild rant that is full of bitterness, anger, and resentment. In most cases, the hearers do not know how to respond helpfully without making things worse for the victim and themselves—worse for the victims because they present themselves in such a bad light, and worse for the hearers because the complaint evokes their own unacknowledged sense of shame. So they clam up and stew in their shame.

The best that our society offers to those who have been shamed is the help of cognitive therapy from well-trained psychologists. While that may help them to discover the reasons for their shame, understand its impact on them, and find ways to cope with it, it requires them to help themselves, as best they can, with various kinds of self-affirmation that aim to bolster their self-esteem. But no matter how skilled they are, cognitive therapists cannot free them from their shame and undo its destructive impact on them. By their therapy they can, at best, provide damage control.

In contrast to these self-help measures, God has actually provided a set of seven psalms to His people who are victims of abuse, victims who are otherwise locked up in their shame and disabled by it. They are Psalms 25, 31, 35, 40, 69, 70, and 71.[55] They belong to a larger class of psalms that are called psalms of lament, or—more accurately, in my opinion—psalms of complaint, by which

54 A whinger is a chronic whiner or moaner.

55 Two other psalms may also be included: Psalm 6, if verse 10 is taken as a wish rather than a hopeful statement, and Psalm 109, if we take verses 6–19 as a quotation of what the psalmist's enemies have to say.

people unload their troubles on God and ask Him for help from them. While some other psalms also touch on the issue of shame in passing,[56] these psalms focus on it as their main concern. They are distinguished by two stock appeals: "Let me not be put to shame" or a paraphrase of it,[57] and "Let the wicked be put to shame" or a paraphrase of it.[58] It is telling that both these appeals are not addressed to God as direct requests but as wishes that say what the psalmists would like to happen.[59] While the appeal to God to save the shamed person from the full fallout from it is backed by further specific requests for help, the appeal for God to shame those who have shamed the psalmist is usually explicated by further wishes for Him to let them suffer the disgrace that they had intended to inflict on their victim.

Apart from these appeals, the psalms of shame vary widely and significantly. They do have a similar orientation and purpose, but each is different in its own way. That should alert us to the danger of generalization. Just as each person is unique in character, so shame affects each of us differently. So, for example, a practical person will be most harmed and best helped by what is done to him or her. An emotional person experiences shame differently than an imaginative person. And so on. The seven psalms of shame therefore encourage us to consider each person, and ourselves, personally with our own experience rather than generally as typical cases.

---

56 See Psalms 6:10; 14:6; 22:5; 34:5; 37:19; 44:7, 15; 53:5; 74:21; 86:17; 89:45; 119:6, 31, 46, 78, 80, 116; 120.

57 Psalms 25:2, 20; 31:1, 17a; 71:1. This is replaced in 69:6 by an appeal that those who hope in God will not be put to shame through the victim of shame. This appeal is not included in Psalms 35, 40, and 70.

58 Psalms 25:2b–3 (if verse 3 is taken as a wish rather than a declaration); 31:17b; 35:4; 40:14–15; 70:2–3; 71:13. This is not included in Psalm 69.

59 In Hebrew grammar, the speaker in the psalm uses first- or third-person verbal forms that express a wish rather than a request or command.

They call for personal empathy rather than impersonal care.

An Exercise in Empathy

All the psalms of shame appeal to God for deliverance from shame in what resembles a civil suit for defamation in our legal system. In these, people who have been severely defamed lodge a suit, with God as the supreme Judge, for vindication and the award of damages against those who have done the shaming (Psalm 35:23–24). All other attempts by the shamed to clear their name have failed. They have, in fact, been counterproductive. They have led to worse attacks from their opponents, who have tried to intimidate and silence, discredit and disable them. So an appeal to God is their last resort, their final hope for the restoration of their honor and social reputation.

The resemblance of these psalms to suits for defamation helps us to understand a theologically puzzling and morally offensive part of them: the apparent demand for revenge, a demand that seems to contradict the biblical teaching that vengeance belongs to God and the consequent prohibition of personal retribution.[60] That lust for revenge seems to be encouraged and sanctioned by their vivid, angry, emotionally charged appeals for retribution.[61] But careful examination of them shows that they resemble a recent innovation in our courts of law. I refer to their provision for a victim impact statement from victims of crime who otherwise have no say in the legal proceedings. In these statements, the victims

60 These are commonly called "imprecations" or "maledictions," which imply that they are curses spoken against the offender.

61 See Psalms 31:17–18; 35:4–7; 69:22–28.

do not tell the judge how to punish the offender but present their point of view to the judge and the whole court. They tell how they feel about what they have suffered and how the situation has damaged them and their families; they may also tell how they regard the offender and how they would like him to be punished.

By the appeals for retribution in these psalms, the shamed person acknowledges his angry desire for revenge for what he has suffered and his emotional compulsion to gain relief from its pain by making the offender suffer what he has suffered. Those who are shamed may know that this is not how they should feel or what they should do. But this is how they actually feel. These appeals express what is otherwise repressed and unexpressed. They confess the hateful, hurtful desire for revenge and appeal to God to relieve them by avenging them instead. The victims of shame thereby forfeit their right to avenge themselves. Once it has been referred to God, they cannot reclaim it and exercise it for themselves. They thereby get rid of the urge for revenge. They have no need to hold onto their slights and use them to justify themselves and their hatred for those who have wronged them.

Yet, while the speaker in these psalms appeals to God as Judge, his appeal is much more personal, intimate, and passionate than that of a rational, formal legal suit. The appeal is to Him as God (Psalms 25:2; 31:14; 35:23, 24; 40:5; 71:4, 12), who has redeemed the speaker (31:5) and has appointed him as His personal servant, His minister (31:16; 35:27; 69:17). His appeals to God for help are therefore much more personal than a legal suit for defamation in a court of law. These are prayers from the heart that are addressed to the heart of God. They are also implicitly communal—but unobtrusively so! The victim of abuse belongs to "the great congregation" (35:18; 40:9), the liturgical community of God's people who gather in His presence in His holy temple to "seek" Him in prayer and praise (40:16; 69:32). Those who have been abused are not excluded from the congregation but are part of it. The psalmist therefore speaks of himself together with them as "us" and the Lord as "our God" (40:3, 5). He regards them directly as devout colleagues (31:23–24) and prays that they will not be shamed through himself (69:6) but rejoice with him in his deliverance (35:27; 40:16). Yet that is incidental. They, as it were, eavesdrop on him as he prays.

I must admit that the personal orientation of these psalms makes me uncomfortable about how I have so far been speaking of them. They are, after all, not literary texts that I may analyze to discover what I can about the nature of shame. They are prayers that are meant to be prayed. They challenge me to exercise discreet empathy as I pay attention to them and am privy to a heart that is poured out to God before me. They invite me to listen in on the prayer of a shamed person who breaks his silence and speaks to God about himself and his experience of shame. As I listen in with all my heart and soul and mind, I am drawn in and encouraged to join with the psalmist by praying for him and others like him. And perhaps too—then and only then—for myself and my largely unacknowledged shame!

Despite the personal character of these psalms, the speaker remains unnamed. It may be King David, since they are all ascribed to him except 71,[62] or Jesus, the Son of David and David's royal heir. It may also be any shamed person, or every shamed soul. Whoever the speaker may be, these psalms require me to stand in the shoes of others who have been shamed and to pray with them. That is what they require of us. In our common prayer, everyone who has been shamed will no longer be isolated in shame but will stand in communion with all of us. There will no longer be the separation of "me" from "them" before God; there will be only "us."

With all this in mind, I now invite you to join me with a hypothetical exercise in empathy that is couched as an interview with the victim of shame who we meet in the seven psalms of shame. The aim of this "interview" is to hear his story of deliverance from shame.

A Story of Shame

Who has shamed you?

> That is hard to say. It feels as if almost everyone is out to shame me. I could name a few people, but I suspect that most of them have been put up to it, or else simply went along with the crowd. Only God knows who they are and what they have done (Psalm 69:19). All I know is that a lot of people have attacked me and still attack me, openly by how they treat me, or secretly by what they say about me behind my back and secretly plot to do to me. I know that they are set to shame

62 Even that psalm is ascribed to David in the Greek translation of the Old Testament. This ascription to David shows that all people, whatever their rank or status in society, are prone to shame and in need of vindication.

me and have succeeded in shaming me publicly, so much so that my former acquaintances flee from me when they see me (31:11) and my own brothers shun me (69:8). They are a faceless mob of liars and mockers who attack me and others like me (35:19–21), a whispering crowd that plots to destroy me (31:13), a crowd of "wicked" people who treat me and other "righteous" people with contempt (31:17–18). Like hunters, they set hidden "nets" to trap me for my downfall and ruin (25:15; 31:4; 35:7–8). I feel like a single defenseless soldier surrounded by a large, well-armed army (35:1–3), a heartbroken person with nobody to pity and comfort me (69:20). So I won't and can't mince words about them. These nameless people are "my enemies" (25:2; 31:15; 69:14; 71:10), "my foes" and "adversaries" who are set on destroying me (31:11; 35:19; 69:19). But it's even worse than that! A single ringleader seems to be behind them, my archenemy who eggs them all on, my main "enemy" (31:8), a "wicked" one who has me in his "unjust and cruel" grasp (71:4).[63] If only I knew who he is and who they are, so that I could confront them and have it out with them. But whoever they are, they seem to be intent on shaming me.

Why are they so intent on shaming you?

I honestly don't know why, even though I would dearly like to discover the reason for their attacks on me. I don't know what I have done to account for their poisonous desire to shame

63 In Psalm 109:6, this archenemy is called "a wicked man," "an accuser" [Satan], my adversary, who, like the others who accuse me (Psalms 38:20; 71:13; 109:20, 29), stands beside me in God's court to prosecute me. The term "accuser" is used as the proper name for the devil in 1 Chronicles 21:1; Job 1:6, 7, 8, 9, 12; 2:1, 2, 3, 4, 6, 7; Zechariah 3:1, 2.

me. The more I try to pin it down, the more elusive it becomes. They have no valid reason to act treacherously against me (Psalm 25:3). They have no reason to be my foes (35:19). Without any valid cause, they hate me (35:19; 69:4) and try to destroy me (35:7). Don't get me wrong! It is not as if I am completely blameless. I have no reason to be self-righteous. I know that I have sinned against God (69:5), and I acknowledge that my sins weigh heavy on me, sapping my strength and darkening my heart, so that I don't see how they have affected me (31:10; 40:12). But that's between God and me! I know that He has promised to atone for my sin and pardon me because He is a God of mercy and goodness (Exodus 34:6–7). That's why I ask Him to "forgive all my sins" (Psalm 25:18) and "pardon my guilt" for His name's sake (25:11). That's why I ask Him to remember me rather than the sins of my youth (25:7). Even though my enemies accuse me, they don't call me to account for my sins before God, so that I could turn to God to judge me and ask Him to acquit me. Instead, they are false witnesses who accuse me publicly and maliciously of crimes, such as theft, that I have never done (35:11, 20–21; 69:4). Yet even though it is unclear why they want to shame me, their motivation is obvious to me from how they treat me. They hate me intently and violently (25:19; 35:19; 69:4). Their hatred of me inflames their malice against me. So they are like secret assassins who "seek after my life" (35:4; see 70:2a); they aim to destroy my soul, my self-esteem, my sense of self, so that they gain power over me (40:14).[64] They seek evil against me; they set out to harm me by what they do and say (71:13, 24). They "devise evil against me" (35:4). When they succeed in that, they "delight in my hurt" (70:2b); they "exult over me" when they have overpowered me (25:2); they "rejoice over me" (35:19, 24) and "rejoice at my calamity" (35:26). Since they watch out to take my life, they plot together to attack me when I am most vulnerable because they reckon that God has forsaken me (71:10–11). Then they band together to rejoice over me when I stumble (35:15). They therefore try to prove how great they are (35:25–26). That is rather revealing because it gives me some inkling about why they are so intent on shaming me. I endure their scorn and shame for God's sake (69:7). It seems to me that the insults of those who insult God fall on me because of my devotion to Him and His house, His place of worship for me and all His people (69:9).

How has this affected you?

I feel afflicted, put down, humiliated, and oppressed.[65] All the malicious attempts to disgrace me have taken a heavy toll on me. They make me very sad (31:10). They have devastated me physically, mentally, and emotionally. They have filled me with deep anguish and distress (25:17; 31:7, 9; 69:17). My enemies have unleashed a torrent of verbal abuse on me with their outright lies (31:18; 69:4); deceptive, poisonous words of accu sation and criticism (35:20); and baseless reproaches that have

64 The same Hebrew word, *nephesh*, is used for the soul, or the self, or the life of a person.

65 See Psalms 25:16; 35:10; 40:17; 69:29; 70:5, where the Hebrew adjective *ani* has this range of meanings.

set out to discredit me and destroy my reputation (69:20).[66] When they slander me, it is as if they bite me with their teeth and tear me to pieces like lions (35:15–17), so that they can devour me (35:25). All this has broken my heart (69:20). I cry my eyes out, overwhelmed as I am with grief and pain and sorrow (31:9–10). I am exhausted from crying out aloud with a parched throat and eyes that have been dimmed by waiting for God to save me (69:3). I am in despair because I have no one to pity and comfort me (69:20). I can best describe how I feel with some stark images that depict my sorry state. It is as if my bones have dissolved and lost their strength (31:10). I am like a broken pot that can't be put together again; I am forgotten by everyone as if I were already dead (31:12). It is as if I am about to drown in deep water that comes right up to my neck or am about to sink in soft mud without reaching any foothold at the bottom of it (69:1–2, 14–15). But worst of all, I am all alone and lonely (25:16) because God seems far from me or, perhaps even, fast asleep (35:22–23). I have worn myself out with crying out to Him and waiting for Him to help me (69:3).

Why then do you ask for help from God?

Quite simply, because He is "my God" (25:2; 31:14; 35:23, 24; 40:5; 71:12). I have found that most people can't help me, and if they can, they don't want to. They may sympathize with me, but that is not enough! I can't even help myself. So I turn to God instead. He is "my help and my deliverer" (40:17; 70:5); He

66 Reproaches blame and taunt people for their supposed faults and failures in order to treat them with contempt and discredit them. See also Psalms 31:11; 69:7, 9, 10, 19, 20; 71:13.

is "my hope; my trust" (71:5); He is "my rock and my fortress" (31:3); He is my "rock of refuge," "my rock and my fortress" (71:7). Best of all, since He is a "faithful God" who has "redeemed me," I know that I can rely on Him and commit myself to Him (31:5). I can be sure of Him because of His covenant with His people and commitment to them with His promise of mercy and grace, "steadfast love and faithfulness" (25:10; 40:11; 69:16). I can rely on His righteousness to save me from my shame (71:2, 15, 16, 17, 24). That's why I trust in Him (25:2; 31:6, 14; 71:5), call on Him (31:17), take refuge in Him (25:20; 31:3–5), and wait on Him in hope for His help (25:3, 5, 21; 31:24; 40:1; 69:3, 6, 20).

What help do you hope to get from God?

My hope is summed up best in this simple prayer (Psalm 70:1):

> Make haste, O God, to deliver me!
> O LORD, make haste to help me!

I plead with God to deliver me (25:20; 31:2, 15; 69:14; 70:1; 71:2). Since I have been shamed by my enemies and face the prospect of further shaming from them, I want God to break their hold on me and deliver me from physical and verbal abuse, from the ongoing impact of that abuse on me, from further abuse, and from the sense of shame that I feel from their contempt for me. So I ask God to turn to me (69:16) and be gracious to me (31:9), to pay attention to me (31:2; 71:2) and answer me (69:13, 16, 17). I ask Him to remember me

(25:7), to consider my distressful humiliation (25:18–19) and free me from it (25:17). I ask Him to fight for me against my enemies with His assurance of salvation (35:1–3), to rescue and to save me from them (31:2; 35:17; 69:1; 71:2), to ransom and redeem me from captivity by them (69:18). Not just once or occasionally, but daily and continually, I hope and pray and praise Him for my deliverance (71:3, 6, 14).[67] Above all else, I ask Him to vindicate me so that the burden of shame is lifted from me (35:22–25) and His face will once again shine on me with light and warmth, grace and favor, approval and acceptance, blessing and peace (31:16). That's what I want most of all. It will show me and my opponents that God is pleased with me and delights in my welfare (35:27).

What do you hope to gain from your deliverance from shame?

This may surprise you, but my main concern is not for the restoration of my status, honor, and self-esteem. In fact, my experience of shame has taught me how fragile my soul is if its sense of worth rests on social evaluation and approval. I have unexpectedly learned how little my reputation matters apart from God and His approval of me. I now know that my honor, my glory, comes from honoring God for His goodness and mercy, His faithfulness and steadfast love. That's why I don't want people to say how great I am but how great God is (35:27; 40:16; 70:4).[68] I don't want people to praise me or

67 The Hebrew word that I translated as "continually" is also used for regular performance of the Divine Service each morning and evening (Exodus 29:38–39, 42).

68 Note the mention of magnifying God in 69:30.

others like me, but only God. Yet that is not something new for me. In fact, even when I was most shamed by my enemies, I never stopped praising God (71:6b, 8). I have always been devoted to praising the Lord and singing a new song of praise to Him with each new answer to my cries for help (40:1–3). But now I vow to keep on praising Him for all His amazing deeds and His incomparable help for me and all His people (40:5). I promise that I will once again rejoice in Him and His salvation when He once again delivers me from those who set out to shame me (31:7–8; 35:10); I will bless Him with amazement for His miraculous protection (31:19–22) and offer a song of thanksgiving for my salvation (69:29–30). I will continue to wait for God and praise Him more and more all day long for all His mighty works (71:14–16). Since God has taught me from my youth to proclaim His wondrous deeds, I want Him to be with me until I am old, so that I can proclaim His power and might to the next generation by telling them how He raises me up from the lowest places and comforts me (71:17–21). I will keep on praising God with music and song for His faithfulness and righteousness in shaming those who have tried to harm me (71:22–24).[69]

So I rejoice in God even as I lament my plight. My experience of shame has backfired on my enemies in their desire to silence me (71:17–20),[70] because my deliverance from shame has confirmed my lifelong resolve to be a praise singer (71:6) and

69 I take 71:19–21 as the content of the proclamation.

70 If we take 71:13 as the nearest antecedent for "them" in 71:16, the praise of God's righteousness is also addressed to those who seek to harm the psalmist with their false accusations.

filled my whole life with praise (71:8). The result of my deliverance is my reorientation back to God. My shame turned me in on myself so fully that I became obsessed with myself and my sorry plight. It robbed me of my joy, my cheerfulness, and my gladness. I became self-absorbed in uncertainty and suspicion, fear and despair. But God's promised deliverance has extroverted and reoriented me. It has taken me out of myself and fixed my attention on Him and His faithful people. Now my main wish is that those who hear the song of my deliverance from shame will stand in awe of the Lord and put their trust in Him (40:3).[71] My most ardent desire is that those who hear how the Lord has saved me will rejoice in Him and magnify Him for my vindication (35:27; 40:16). That then will give me even greater cause to praise the Lord for His righteousness and my vindication (35:28).

Afterword

The seven psalms of shame get us to look backward and forward. They get us to look backward to consider how we have been shamed. But they also get us to look forward from our shame to our deliverance from it by Jesus. While we would like to be freed from shame once and forever, they paint a different, much more complex prospect for us. They show that we are caught up in a recurring cycle of shame and deliverance, a good cycle that opens us to further and fuller deliverance. So now, in conclusion, I would like to mention four things that they foreshadow for us: the identity

71 This sentence can be taken as both a statement and a wish.

of our enemies, Christ's solidarity with us in our shame, the ultimate purpose of our appeal to God to shame our enemies, and our deliverance from shame by Jesus.

First, Jesus shows us that we, spiritually, have no human enemies. The devil and the demons are the enemies that are intent on shaming us. The devil is our true enemy (Matthew 13:39; Luke 10:19). He is the enemy behind all those who seem to be our enemies. As is evident from his name, he is a "slanderer." Jesus calls him Satan, the Accuser (Matthew 4:10; 12:26; 16:23; Mark 4:15; Luke 10:18; 11:18; 13:16; 22:31). But Jesus has disarmed Satan, together with all the demons, and put them to open shame by His death on the cross (Colossians 2:15). We therefore have little or nothing to fear from them.

Second, Jesus suffered undeserved shame with us and for us by His shameful crucifixion. As He hung on the cross, He was derided by people who were passing by (Matthew 27:39–40), mocked by the religious leaders (27:41–43), and taunted by the two men who were crucified with Him (27:44).[72] All that for our benefit! In Romans 15:2–5, Paul therefore teaches that Jesus prays Psalm 69 for us. Jesus joins David and everyone else who has been ridiculed and dishonored for the sake of the Lord, the God of hosts (Psalm 69:6). He echoes their bold complaint to God and says, "The reproaches of those who reproach You have fallen on Me" (Psalm 69:9; see also Romans 15:3). He bears our shame and prays for us so that we can pray this psalm and the other six psalms of shame together with Him. His solidarity with us in our shame encourages

72 One of them eventually changed his mind and defended Him (Luke 23:39–41).

us to hope in God for our deliverance and praise Him for His help (Romans 15:4–13). When Jesus teaches His apostles on the night before His death about the world's hatred of Him and them (John 15:18–25), Jesus says that this fulfills the complaint in Psalms 35:19 and 69:4: "They hated Me without a cause." He therefore identifies Himself and each of us with the speaker in these psalms. In fact, He says that those who hate His servants persecute them "on account of My name" (John 15:21), just because they are His servants. Jesus therefore prays these psalms of shame for His disciples and together with them.

Third, something unexpected and surprising is included with the appeal in Psalm 70:2–3 for God's judgment on those who have shamed David. David does not just want his enemies to be shamed as he has been shamed; he wants them to "be turned back because of their shame."[73] This phrase is usually taken to mean that they turn back from shaming him and recoil from what they have done. But this phrase can also be translated as "in their shame" or "with their shame." If that is so, then David appeals to God for them to be put to shame, so that, like the prodigal son in Luke 15, they will "turn back" to God in repentance and be restored to life with God.

Fourth, when we look to Jesus and rely on Him for our vindication, our faces will never be ashamed (Psalm 34:5). We may be shamed by what is done to us. But we will never be put to shame, because we still have Jesus' unequivocal approval. So those who try to shame us can never ever make us ashamed of ourselves and

73 The original Hebrew commonly refers to repentance as turning away from sin to God for His pardon (e.g., Nehemiah 9:26; Jeremiah 3:1, 7, 10, 12, 14, 22; Joel 2:13).

Jesus. No matter how much they censure and abuse us, we have no reason to feel ashamed, because Jesus is our rock and refuge. He covers our shame with His righteousness and holiness. We know that He will hear our appeal and will take it up for us by praying:

> [1]To You, O LORD, I lift up my soul.
>
> [2]O my God, in You I trust;
> let me not be put to shame;
> let not my enemies exult over me.
> [3]Indeed, none who wait for You shall be put to shame;
> they shall be ashamed who are wantonly treacherous.
> (Psalm 25:1–3)

Questions for Reflection and Discussion

1. Is there anything in this chapter that you would like to discuss?

2. Read Psalm 25 and work out how it applies to you in your experience of shame so that you discover God's way to find your way through it.

3. How do the seven psalms of shame help those who have been shamed by injustice to deal with their hurt and anger as well as the urgent need for revenge and vindication?

4. How do these psalms help us to seek justice without dealing unjustly with those who have wronged us?

5. Why is it so surprising and helpful to discover that Jesus Himself prayed these psalms?

CHAPTER FIVE

The Way of the Cross

Behold, the Lamb of God,
who takes away the sin of the world!

(John 1:29)

Picture the following scenario: A man suffers from a chronic sense of shame and worthlessness that goes back to his rejection as an unwanted child by his parents. This rejection has been confirmed many times in his subsequent experiences of abuse, which have increased his shame. By lashing out at those who have hurt him, he has added guilt to his shame. The details do not matter here, even though they are all significant and they all make him feel even more ashamed of himself.

After keeping the pain of his shame bottled up deep inside himself, he finally finds a sympathetic friend who listens to his angry tale of woe without criticizing him. He concludes his outburst by saying, "This is killing me. Can you please help me?" His friend says that she will do her best to help by trying to understand him sympathetically. But the shame-stricken man retorts that she could not possibly understand him because she has not experienced what he has suffered.

That encounter encourages him to visit a therapist who has a record of being very helpful to people like him. As the therapist listens attentively and sympathetically, he shows that he understands the man's chronic sense of shame and tells him what he can do to manage its severity. After many sessions, the shamed man tells his therapist that these strategies do not help him at all because, try as he may, he is quite unable to fix his shame. He needs someone who will not only understand and share his shame but will also pick it up and get rid of it for him. The therapist admits that he cannot do that. In fact, no one can.

In desperation, the man goes to a pastor and asks him whether he can get rid of the shame for him. He, too, says that he is unable to remove his shame—but Jesus can!

I know that this scenario is rather simplistic and glib. But it serves to introduce this pivotal chapter, in which I shall do my best to unpack something utterly amazing, something that surprised even the people who were familiar with the teaching of the Old Testament about God's promise of deliverance from shame. The surprise is how God accomplishes this for us by the sacrificial death of His Son. He delivers us from shame by His endurance of shame—the shame of His rejection and unjust crucifixion. He therefore swaps places with us. In that great exchange, He bears our shame and gives us His glory, He bears our guilt and gives us His righteousness, He bears our impurity and gives us His purity, He bears our unworthiness and gives us His holiness, He bears our death and gives us His life.

From Shame to Shame

The life of Jesus was lived under the shadow of shame. Both of His human parents were of royal descent at a time when the Jewish monarchy had long ceased to exist and Judea had become a minor province in the Roman Empire. From a human point of view, He was conceived by an unmarried young girl called Mary, who was betrothed to a humble carpenter in an insignificant town remote from the centers of power. The shame of His illegitimate conception was covered up by her innocent fiancé, who refused to divorce her but married her, even though he was not the father of the child (Matthew 1:18–19, 23–24). Jesus was not born in the home of His parents in Nazareth but in a stable in Bethlehem, where He had a manger as His cradle rather than a proper bed (Luke 2:7). He spent the first stage of His life with His parents in Egypt as a refugee to escape slaughter by King Herod, who served as a paranoid puppet for the Romans. Jesus, Mary, and Joseph stayed there until the death of the king (Matthew 2:13–22). Then His parents took Him back to the insignificant village of Nazareth. At the end of this stage of His life, He went to be baptized by John as if He Himself were a sinner who needed to be freed from sin (Matthew 3:13–15).

After His Baptism, Jesus became a homeless, itinerant religious preacher and teacher to His own people, even though He had no normal religious education nor any formal theological credentials. His work began with some success as crowds of people came to hear Him. But His initial success aroused opposition and rejection from the people who mattered most, the religious leaders of the

Jews, who turned against Him and plotted to execute Him. His religious mission ended largely in failure. Even the crowds of people who followed Him deserted Him, until He was left with only twelve disciples (John 6:60–69). Yet even one of them betrayed Him (6:70–71), and all of them deserted Him when He was arrested by a mob of thugs who had been sent out by the religious leaders of His own people (Matthew 26:55–56).

Then came His irregular trial in a hastily convened religious court on trumped-up charges, with false witnesses who could not even agree on what crimes He supposedly had committed. This court judged that He deserved to be put to death for blasphemy because He Himself admitted that He was the Messiah, God's royal Son (Matthew 26:62–66). Since the Jews were not allowed to carry out that sentence, they then referred the case to the Roman governor, Pilate, on the pretext that Jesus was planning to lead a political rebellion against Rome as the King of the Jews. Even though Pilate knew that Jesus was innocent, he agreed to have Him executed to avoid a riot and to cover his own back with the Roman emperor. Then, after that irregular trial, Jesus was crucified, together with two other criminals, and died a shameful death. He was in every way a victim of shameful injustice. From a human point of view, His work and His life ended in utter failure. He lived under the shadow of shame and died in shame, the shame of crucifixion.

The Pain of Shame

When people consider the suffering of Jesus, they usually think of the brutal violence and physical pain that Jesus had to endure.

That has been impressed on many Christians by the sermons they have heard in Lent and on Good Friday, sermons that have often emphasized the brutality and savagery of Jesus' death. This impression has been reinforced in the popular imagination by the graphic depiction of His beating and crucifixion in the popular film *The Passion of the Christ* (2004). To be sure, the accounts of His suffering in the Gospels do mention three instances of physical abuse that was inflicted on Him before His crucifixion. Some members of the Jewish court and some Roman soldiers hit Him in His face (Matthew 26:67; John 19:3), and the Roman governor, Pilate, had Him scourged with a multi-lashed whip that had pieces of metal and bone embedded in it (Matthew 27:26; Mark 15:15). But that is all! What's more, the accounts of His Passion do not even focus on the agony of the crucifixion. So, for example, Mark simply says, "And they crucified Him" (15:24). The most graphic physical aspect of His crucifixion that is mentioned is the piercing of His side by a spear after His death (John 19:34). So, surprisingly, the Gospels do not dwell on the physical pain of Jesus. Instead, they focus our attention on the shame that He suffered by His crucifixion. It set out to shame Him and discredit His social, moral, and spiritual standing.

Jesus was shamed by being rejected and abandoned by the people who should have supported Him. The Jewish leadership, which consisted of the chief priests and the members of the Jewish religious court, rejected Him and decided to have Him put to death. Egged on by the priests, the people turned on Him at His trial before Pilate and chose to have Him crucified rather than Barabbas, a convicted terrorist who had been found guilty of murder in an uprising against the Roman government. Judas, one of Jesus' twelve disciples, betrayed Him for thirty silver coins. Even His other eleven disciples abandoned Him. When Jesus was arrested by a band of thugs, the disciples all left Him in the lurch and ran away to escape being arrested with Him. His chief disciple, Peter, dissociated himself from his master and disowned Him three times. But worst of all, Jesus was even abandoned by His heavenly Father. After He had hung for three long hours of darkness on the cross, He cried out with a loud voice, "My God, My God, why have You forsaken Me?" (Matthew 27:46; Mark 15:34). This is the first verse of Psalm 22, in which God's royal deputy, David, laments that God has forsaken him by allowing him to be scorned by mankind and despised by his own people (22:1–8). That experience of abandonment by God was the worst of all the shame that Jesus suffered at His crucifixion.

Jesus was also shamed by His unjust condemnation as an evildoer. This is emphasized by the accounts of His Passion in all the Gospels. They focus more attention on His trial than on His crucifixion. His rushed trial proceeded in two stages: the first before the Jewish religious court, which was convened and led by the high priest, and the second before Pilate, the Roman governor, whose task it was to administer justice in Judea. Both trials were marked by the exercise of gross injustice. The aim of the Jewish court was to confirm its prior decision to put Jesus to death (Mark 14:55). But, despite their machinations, they found no legal evidence for their decision because their case rested on the unreliable testimony of false witnesses who could not even agree with one another. As the last resort, the high priest got Jesus to incriminate Himself by asking Him whether He was the Christ, the Son of God (14:61). Jesus therefore was condemned to death for blasphemy (14:63–64).

Since the Jewish authorities had no authority to execute anybody (John 18:31), the case was referred to Pilate for confirmation and enactment on the pretext that Jesus was a king in waiting and potential rebel against the Roman emperor (Luke 23:2). Luke reports that Pilate declared three times that Jesus was innocent (23:4, 14, 22).[74] Under immense pressure, Pilate caved in to save his own skin and agreed to have Jesus executed, even though he himself was so convinced that Jesus was innocent that he washed his hands publicly to shift the blame for the unjust death of Jesus back onto the Jewish leaders (Matthew 27:24). Jesus' innocence was acknowledged by Pilate's wife (27:19) and confirmed by the centurion who supervised His execution (Luke 23:47). Jesus therefore was accused, condemned, and sentenced to death for no crime, but only for His status as God's Son. By His condemnation and crucifixion, He was treated not just as an evildoer; He was also ranked with the worst of all criminals. And that despite His innocence! What could be more shameful and unjust than that?

Jesus was also shamed by the mockery that He suffered. He was not just abused verbally by the crowd of ignorant people who showed their unjustified contempt for Him. He was also ridiculed by people who were familiar with the Scriptures and knew what He had said and done. They mocked Him as a deluded man who

74 See also John 18:38; 19:4.

imagined that He would be a king, and not just any king but the promised Messiah, God's King, God's royal Son.

Jesus was subjected to three kinds of mockery. First, He was ridiculed as a false prophet. Some of the temple guard and some of the priests blindfolded Him, slapped Him, and demanded that He prove His claim to be a prophet by disclosing who had struck Him. Second, before they crucified Him, the soldiers ridiculed Him as a would-be messiah who imagined that He would reign as the King of the Jews by staging a mock coronation with Him. They put a purple cloak over Him, set a crown of thorns on His head, hailed Him as the King of the Jews, touched His head with a reed rather than a scepter, spat on Him, and knelt down in mock homage before Him. Third, as Jesus hung on the cross, He was mocked for claiming to be God's Son, the Savior of God's people by three groups of people: the bystanders, the religious leaders, and those who were crucified with Him all challenged Him to prove His divine status and power by coming down from the cross and saving Himself from death.

Ironically true for both Him and us was the sarcastic taunt of the well-educated religious leaders: "He saved others; He cannot save Himself" (Matthew 27:42; Mark 15:31). He chose to use His divine status and power to save others rather than Himself by His innocent suffering and death. He was forsaken by others and by God so that we will never be forsaken by our heavenly Father. He was innocently condemned to death in order to pardon and free us from sin. He was humbled by the mockery of His divine status and identity as God's Son so that we could share in His Sonship as children of God.

Enduring the Cross

We would expect God to deliver us from shame by shaming those who have shamed us. We would expect Him to exercise His superior power to defeat them, like the Allies who defeated Hitler in World War II. But God did not go that way in His commission and mission for His Son. Instead, He chose the way of suffering and endurance, the way to glory through humiliation, the way to joy through pain, the way to strength through weakness, the way to victory through apparent defeat. That is how the author of Hebrews describes the amazing turnabout that occurred through the death of God's Son in an exhortation to us to go along with Jesus on His way, which passes through the shame of His crucifixion to the joy of His resurrection and the glory of His ascension:

> *1*Let us run with endurance the race that is set before us,
> *2*looking to Jesus, the founder and perfecter[75] of our faith, who for the joy that was set before Him endured the cross, despising the shame, and is seated[76] at the right hand of the throne of God. (Hebrews 12:1–2)

The key word here is "endurance," the endurance of the cross by Jesus and our endurance in looking to Him.[77]

In my youth, I enjoyed athletics. Even though I was best at sprinting, I enjoyed the challenge of cross-country races most, because they tested my endurance. I discovered that for me the key

---

75 Or "author and finisher." He is the perfecter of our faith because He brings us and it to its goal.

76 Here "seated" refers to His enthronement beside His royal Father as coregent with Him. See Psalm 110:1; Matthew 19:28; Mark 16:19; Ephesians 1:20; Hebrews 1:3; 8:1; 10:12.

77 In Greek, this word combines the notion of endurance with patience and persistence, confident courage and steadfast expectation.

to success was to fix my eyes on the lead runner rather than the finish line. I would let that runner set the pace, and I would follow close behind him in his slipstream. When I faced a headwind, he would shield me from it and pull me along behind him. If I was running in a team with a friend in a slow race, we would take turns in setting a good pace. My success depended on my endurance, and my endurance depended on taking the race step by step after the leader rather than thinking about how far I still had to go. That made it easier to run the race because, no matter how tired I was, I could always take one or two more steps.

Jesus is not just the lead runner in the race of faith. He is its founder and perfecter. It begins, continues, and ends with Him. It is a race through the darkness into the light, an invisible race with an invisible goal, for in the race of faith, we cannot see exactly where we are in it or where we are going. We are aware only of Him and those who are running with us. He sets the course for us through a dangerous, hostile world, where it is easy to stumble and get lost. The point of the race is to reach the goal together with all the other runners rather than to reach it first. In this race, we are called to fix our eyes and ears on Jesus and to endure the shame together with Him. He pioneered the way for us by His shameful death on the cross, where those who were hostile to Him and who despised Him did all they could to shame Him into dropping out from the race.

He endured His crucifixion by despising the shame that was inflicted on Him by those who were hostile to Him. He did not pay them back by despising them and treating them with contempt.

Instead, He asked His heavenly Father to forgive them. Peter describes how Jesus endured His suffering in this way:

> [23]When He was reviled, He did not revile in return; when He suffered, He did not threaten, but continued entrusting Himself to Him who judges justly. [24]He Himself bore our sins in His body on the tree, that we might die to sin and live to righteousness. (1 Peter 2:23–24)

Jesus willingly endured the shame of His trial and crucifixion because of the joy that was set before Him after His shameful death. That joyful goal was His resurrection and enthronement at the right hand of His heavenly Father, so that He could intercede for those who were burdened with sin and bring them with Him into His Father's presence. He endured the shame of the cross so that He could bear their guilt and shame and take them with Him from shame into glory. He endured the cross so that they, through their faith in Him, could also endure their shame by fixing their eyes on Him rather than on those who were bent on shaming them for their faith in Him.

In 1 Peter 2:20; 3:14–17; and 4:13–19, Peter distinguishes between three kinds of suffering that correspond with three kinds of shame. First, there is well-deserved suffering from wrongdoing. There is nothing commendable about that at all (2:20a). Then there is the suffering of undeserved abuse for doing what is good and righteous (3:14–17). Peter calls that abuse suffering for the sake of righteousness (3:14). This is commendable and pleasing to God, because, by their good behavior, they shame those who abuse them. What's more, those who are abused for doing good receive

God's approval and blessing as their reward. He protects them from shame and discredits those who abuse them. Last, and by no means least, there is the abuse that Christians suffer because they bear Christ's name and follow Him (4:13–16). Even though they suffer unjust abuse, they have no reason to feel ashamed. Because they share Christ's suffering, they will also eventually share His glory. In fact, they will be blessed by God already now because the Spirit of glory in God rests on them in their suffering (4:14). And that gives them good reason to rejoice, even when they suffer. They have a preview of heavenly glory in their suffering.

The Shame of the Cross

Crucifixion was the worst form of capital punishment for the worst crimes in the Roman Empire. It was a cruel form of execution in which the wrists were nailed to the crossbeam so that they took the full weight of the body. This weight was eased only by the attachment of the feet by nails or rope to a footrest on the main beam. This usually ensured that the crucified person died a slow, excruciatingly painful death. Even worse than that, it was a spectacle that was meant to shame the person who was being executed in a public place, such as beside the main road out of the city, as a warning and example to criminals and enemies of the state. By crucifixion, the political leaders of a community treated criminals and rebels with derision and contempt as worthless outcasts from civilized society. Crucifixion destroyed criminals' reputations so completely that their name would die with them and none would want to be associated with them and their cause. The final verdict on them was that they were useless, worthless people whose unburied bodies were often dumped in the nearest rubbish pit.

The enemies of Jesus wanted to shame Him in the worst possible way they had at their disposal. And shame Him they did! Yet it did not achieve what they intended to accomplish. It was, in fact, counterproductive in three ways. First, Jesus did not resist His crucifixion but endured it willingly, going along with it as He had repeatedly taught His disciples that He would (Matthew 16:21; 17:22–23; 20:17–19; 26:2). His unjust death was the purpose of His human life on earth. It was the will of His heavenly Father for Him (Isaiah 53:10; Matthew 26:39, 42). He "must" do what was "written" about Him by the prophets (Luke 9:22; 18:31). In obedience to His Father, He did not despise His ignorant enemies, who did not know what they were doing (Luke 23:34). He despised the shame associated with that kind of suffering and death, instead regarding it as a mark of God's approval and honor (see Hebrews 12:2). It was the hour of His glorification as the Son of Man and our glorification through Him (John 12:20–26; 13:31–32).

Second, Jesus knew that His life and work would not end at His death but would culminate in the joy that was set before Him after His death with His resurrection and ascension. The author of Hebrews gives us this explanation of the joy that was set before Jesus:

> 9But we see Him who for a little while was made lower than the angels, namely Jesus, crowned with glory and honor because of the suffering of death, so that by the grace of

> God He might taste death for everyone. [10]For it was fitting that He, for whom and by whom all things exist, in bringing many sons to glory, should make the founder of their salvation perfect through suffering. [11]For He who sanctifies and those who are sanctified all have one source.[78] That is why He is not ashamed to call them brothers. . . . [14]Since therefore the children share in flesh and blood, He Himself likewise partook of the same things, that through death He might destroy the one who has the power of death, that is, the devil, [15]and deliver all those who through fear of death were subject to lifelong slavery. (Hebrews 2:9–11, 14–15)

This passage connects the human life, death, resurrection, and ascension of Jesus with our deliverance from the shame of eternal death. By His incarnation, Jesus shared our whole human life cycle from the womb to the tomb so completely as our human brother that He tasted the bitterness of death on our behalf, freed us from slavery to the fear of condemnation to eternal death, joined us together with Himself as members of God's family, shared His holiness with us, and brought us to glory as children of God together with Him. He therefore had no reason to be ashamed of us but was proud to call us His siblings. He covers our shame with His holiness and presents us to God the Father as perfect through His physical union with us (Hebrews 2:13).

Third, the shame of Jesus' crucifixion led to the glory of His enthronement to the highest place of honor and power in heaven and earth (Hebrews 2:9; 12:2). That place was the right-hand side

78 Literally "all are from one."

of God the Father in heaven. In the ancient world, the king's deputy sat on a throne at the right hand of his royal father on ceremonial occasions and in his official capacity as his father's right-hand man, his legal heir and coregent. As second-in-command to his father, he was entrusted with the routine administration of the realm. Since he had open access to the king, he served as a mediator between the king and his citizens. However, Jesus does not just serve as coregent with His heavenly Father; He is also our High Priest who intercedes for us. He gives us access to His Father's grace and favor so that, through Him, we can now receive God's mercy and divine help for all that we need in our life on earth (4:14–16). As our High Priest who has also experienced human temptations, He sympathizes with us in our weakness and shame. He exercises His spiritual power mercifully and graciously by helping us and serving us. He does not put us down but lifts us up, so that through faith we receive all that we need from Him. Just as He once shared our life on earth, He now shares His life in heaven with us here on earth. The joy of all that moved Him to endure the shame of the cross and still moves Him to endure the hostility of sinners against Him (12:1–3).

An Odd Reversal

The story of the nations is marked by revolutions that disrupt governments by upending established orders. In nearly every political revolution, those who are underprivileged and disempowered attempt to displace those who are in power. The have-nots claim what they do not have: power, wealth, and status from those who govern them. Unlike that, Jesus inaugurates a different revolution by His human life, death, and resurrection—a spiritual revolution in which He casts down the mighty from their thrones and exalts the lowly in their lowliness; a revolution downward by which He rules from below rather than above, a new order for human life in a new community with new notions of shame and honor.

Paul explores this great reversal with passionate intensity in 1 Corinthians 1:17–31, talking about the religious implications of Christ's death on the cross for him and for the church in Corinth. He unpacks the paradoxical "word of the cross," a message that contradicts human concepts of political wisdom and spiritual power. For how could a man who had been crucified as a criminal be the righteous, divinely appointed King of heaven and earth? How could a man who has been condemned to death by the Jewish high priest—God's earthly representative—be the Christ whom God had anointed with His Spirit as His holy High Priest and heavenly King? How could the teaching of a discredited dead man save anybody at all?

In 1 Corinthians 1:18–19, Paul recalls God's declaration in Isaiah 29:14 that He would destroy the wisdom and discernment of those who fancied that they were wise. Paul makes this the basis for his confident assertion about the crucifixion of Jesus: "The word of the cross is folly to those who are perishing, but to us who are being saved it is the power of God" (1:18). What a strange kind of power, which looks like utter weakness from a human point of view. The power of God is not shown by its active exercise of coercion and control but in the endurance of suffering by His Son and the proclamation of salvation through faith in Him.

Then, in 1 Corinthians 1:20–25, Paul argues that the word of the cross—the message of Christ crucified for the salvation of the world—contradicts the wisdom of the Jews and Gentiles, the religious ideology of the Jewish community, and the political ideology of the Roman Empire. These believed that their safety and success depended on the active exercise of power: political power for the Gentiles by their obedience to Roman law and spiritual power for the Jews by their obedience to God's Law. They therefore demanded that the invisible God prove His existence and disclose His character through the demonstration of His power by supernatural wisdom or supernatural miracles. But God chose to make Himself known through the folly and weakness of Christ's shameful death by crucifixion (1:16–18). Then, to add insult to injury, God chose to save both Jews and Gentiles through the proclamation of Christ crucified by unsophisticated preachers like Paul and their faith in Christ (1:21).

Since the members of the church in Corinth knew this from their own experience, Paul challenged them to recall what had happened to them and to learn from it (1 Corinthians 1:26–31). Like officials who could understand their status and power from their terms of employment, the Corinthians were to consider their calling, God's choice of them to be His holy children (1:2, 9). They were to recall how God had called them and what He had called them to be when they first heard the Gospel of Jesus, believed in it, and were united with Him by Baptism:

> [26]For consider your calling, brothers: not many of you were wise according to worldly standards, not many were powerful, not many were of noble birth. [27]But God chose what is foolish in the world to shame the wise; God chose what is weak in the world to shame the strong; [28]God chose what is low and despised in the world, even things that are not, to bring to nothing things that are, [29]so that no human being might boast in the presence of God. [30]And because of Him[79] you are in Christ Jesus, who became to us wisdom from God, righteousness and sanctification and redemption, [31]so that, as it is written, "Let the one who boasts, boast in the Lord."[80] (1 Corinthians 1:26–31)

The Jewish and Roman ruling classes of Judea set out to shame Jesus by crucifying Him. They crucified Him because His life and teaching were a threat to their status and hold on power. His crucifixion was meant to show His ignorance and weakness, His worthlessness and insignificance. But that backfired on them. It, in fact, showed how empty their claim to holy wisdom and legitimate power really was.

By the death and resurrection of Jesus, God put the powerful Jewish and Roman leaders to shame by discounting their status, which depended on four key credentials. Their first credential was their power. For the Romans, it was their possession of political power, which came from their military, legal, and administrative ability; for the Jews, it was their spiritual power, which came from

79 Literally, "from Him."

80 See also 2 Corinthians 10:17. This is a paraphrase of God's prophetic admonition in Jeremiah 9:23–24 to the proud, disobedient leaders of His people who relied on their own wisdom, power, and wealth for their safety rather than on God's Word.

their righteousness, holiness, and religiosity. The second credential was their privileged noble birth, with the prestige that came from their hereditary membership in either the religious aristocracy for the Jews or in the landowning political aristocracy for the Romans. The third credential was their wisdom. For the Romans, that came from their education in Greek philosophy and Roman law; for the Jews, it came from their education in the Scriptures and God's Law. Their fourth credential was the position in society that both groups had gained from their power, prestige, and education. Thus, in the final count, their honor and worth depended on their ranking and rating in the social order.

Paul draws an unexpected conclusion from God's choice of socially and politically underprivileged people to shame those who are privileged by calling the former to be His holy people. We would expect Paul to say that God rejected those who were in power and replaced them with those were underprivileged. But that was not God's way. Instead of that, God shamed those who were held to be spiritually powerful, so that no one would be able to boast in His presence (1 Corinthians 1:29). Christ's death on the cross for us puts us all on the same footing before God. In His presence, we are all equally shameful because we all have done wrong and been wronged. We are all equally weak and ignorant. Apart from God, we are all nobodies and have-nots, no matter how significant we may be by the standards of the world that we live in. The crucifixion of Jesus and the message of the cross puts the whole of humanity on ground zero in relation to God. No one has anything to boast about with Him. We all depend on God for everything.

But strangely, that apparent humiliation is the ground for our exaltation, a miracle that Paul compares to God's creation of a new human community from nothing (1 Corinthians 1:28), just as God created the first man from nothing but clay. By putting us all to shame, He delivers us all from shame. That great reversal is all God's doing and giving (1:30–31). By Baptism and through faith in the Gospel of Jesus, God unites us with Jesus and Himself. Jesus is now our brother. He shares Himself and what He has with us. He hands on to us what He receives from His heavenly Father. In Him and through Him, we have "wisdom from God." Yet He does not give us divine wisdom; He is God's wisdom for us. By our union with Him, Jesus does not give us a religious ideology, a system of theological theories and ideas; He does not teach us moral theology, a code of moral laws and a compendium of ethical principles. He gives Himself to us as the embodiment of God's wisdom to save us by what He provides for us. He unites Himself with us and with His heavenly Father.

We receive three things from Jesus as the embodiment of God's wisdom, three things that He offers to save us from shame. First, Jesus is our righteousness. We are justified by God's pardon for our wrongdoing and vindicated by His approval of us. Second, Jesus is our sanctification. He shares His own holiness with us by giving us His Holy Spirit. His holiness covers our shame so completely that we are faultless in God's eyes, secretly already now (1 Corinthians 2:6–11) and manifestly on Judgment Day (1:8). Since we are united with Jesus, God the Father is as pleased with us as He is with Him. Third, Jesus is our redemption. Since He paid the price for our freedom, He now delivers us from the bondage to guilt and shame that we experience by the accusation and condemnation of the devil. He redeems us for life together with Him and His heavenly Father. All that is ours and much more. Yet we never possess it by ourselves apart from Jesus. Since we belong to Him, all that belongs to Him belongs to us (3:21–23).

So we have nothing to boast about (1 Corinthians 1:29). Yet, paradoxically, we have much to boast of in Jesus (1:31). We boast in Him as our Lord because we receive everything from Him. Later on, in 1 Corinthians 4:7, Paul discounts our self-importance and self-promotion with these two withering questions: "What do you have that you did not receive? If then you received it, why do you boast as if you did not receive it?" Just as a pauper married to a millionaire shares the spouse's assets and privileges, we are spiritually enriched and privileged through our union with Jesus.

Life Under the Cross

At this point in my discussion on shame, I had intended to explain how we have received deliverance from shame. But then I realized that neither Jesus nor the writers of the four Gospels teach us about that at all. They don't consider the various kinds of shame and the proper pastoral treatment for them. In fact, Jesus actually has little or nothing to say to His disciples about shame, although He does touch on matters related to it, such as their desire for greatness, concern of public recognition, and pride in their achievements. Yet, without speaking explicitly about shame, Jesus deals with it implicitly again and again in many ways in His encounters with the people that He meets, both people who have done wrong and people who have been wronged.

He engages with them graciously and mercifully, respectfully and gently according to their spiritual needs. He eats and drinks with sexually abused prostitutes and self-righteous Pharisees. He seldom puts down the shamed, and when He does, He puts them down in order to lift them up. He delivers them from their undeserved shame as well as their well-deserved shame by how He regards them and treats them. He saves them by what He says to them and what He does for them. He doesn't follow a set procedure to free them from their entrapment in guilt and shame. He shows that He is not ashamed of them by His contact with them. In all the cases, He gives them something of Himself as a person and encourages them to trust Him to help and save them. He is their redemption. They gain a new self, a new status, and a new sense of worth through Him and what He says to them. They gain confidence and hope from Him.

It is telling that Jesus teaches His disciples about shame only once. His instruction on shame comes at the turning point of His ministry in Mark 8:27–38 and Luke 9:18–27. Both these accounts begin with Peter's confession of faith in Jesus as the Christ. After that, Jesus first tells His disciples about His imminent rejection by the religious leaders, His death by execution, and His subsequent resurrection. Then, in Luke 9:23–27, He gives this instruction on the way of discipleship, addressing it to all disciples rather than just His twelve apostles:

> [23]If anyone would come after Me, let him deny himself and take up his cross daily and follow Me. [24]For whoever would save his life will lose it, but whoever loses his life for My sake[81] will save it. [25]For what does it profit a man if he gains the whole world and loses or forfeits himself? [26]For whoever is ashamed of Me and My words, of him will the Son of Man be ashamed when He comes in His glory and the glory of the Father and of the holy angels. [27]But I tell you truly, there are some standing here who will not taste death until they see the kingdom of God.[82]

In the ancient world—and still in many societies today—honor was held to be like money that can be earned and accumulated. Like money, its value could be assessed in terms of profit and loss. It was gained or lost by the public recognition of a person's advancement or demotion in position and rank. The higher the position, the greater the honor. The lower the position, the greater the shame. By that measure, the people at the bottom of the ladder of honor in the ancient world, such as slaves and criminals, were regarded as worthless nonentities. In contrast to this, Jesus teaches a new way for the assessment of the worth of His disciples, a way in which His cross is the standard for spiritual shame and honor.

The way of discipleship is the way of the cross, the way that Jesus went, the way through the shame of unjust suffering and death by His crucifixion to the glory of His resurrection. It is the way that He went to save people from guilt and shame. It is also

---

81 In Mark 8:35, Jesus adds: "and the gospel's."

82 This most likely refers to the manifestation of Jesus' glory as God's Son to Peter, James, and John in Luke 9:28–32.

the way that He prepared for His disciples to travel through life with Him as their master. In this instruction, Jesus first tells them that discipleship requires three closely connected acts from each of them: to deny themselves, to take up their cross daily, and to follow Him (Luke 9:23). Then He explains why they need to do this, with two warnings and two promises (9:24–27). He warns them of the deadly peril of losing themselves and their lives as well as the even worse peril of being shamed by Jesus; He promises that those who lose themselves and their lives for His sake will gain themselves and eternal life and glory with Him.

Jesus calls on all His disciples to deny themselves. They should not put themselves first in their desire to get their own way and exercise power over others. Instead, they should put Jesus first and listen to what He has to say to them. Self-affirmation and self-protection, self-promotion and self-advancement must be left behind as they obey Jesus and do what He wants them to do. They should trust in Him to save them, care for them, protect them, and honor them. Jesus also calls on them to take up their cross daily by refusing to pay back abuse with abuse and choosing to pay back evil with good. Just as Christ has borne their sins and the sins of the whole world, so He calls them to endure the abuse and shame of those who sin against them. Just as Jesus endured the gauntlet of shame and scorn when He carried His cross on the way to His crucifixion, so they are called to endure all the attacks on them that are meant to shame them for their faith in Jesus and commitment to His Word. They should not expect the world to approve of their faithfulness and honor them for it. Quite simply, Jesus calls them to keep on following Him no matter where they are and no matter what happens to them. They are to follow Him and His Word day by day, because their deliverance from shame depends on Him and what He tells them. His Word is the means by which He supports, empowers, and delivers them.

Jesus explains why His disciples are to follow Him on the shameful way of the cross by speaking of their faithful obedience to Him in terms of ultimate profit and ultimate loss. If they decide to save themselves by forsaking Jesus, going their own way and asserting themselves, they will lose their souls, their true selves, their eternal identity as children of God. Even if they gain power over the whole world, they will end up as spiritually worthless non-entities with no eternal worth. If they are ashamed of Jesus and His saving Word, Jesus will put them to shame in His final judgment; He will disassociate Himself from them and disown them. But if His disciples are willing to lose their old selves and old lives in little daily "deaths" by trusting in Jesus and following Him faithfully, they will gain a new eternal self and a new eternal life of glory with Jesus.

Jesus calls us to follow Him day by day on a lifelong journey of deliverance from shame as He leads us into glory together with Him. As we discover from Hebrews 12:1–2, we follow Him by looking to Him as we run the race of faith with endurance, the race that is set before us, until we stand before Him and His heavenly Father, holy and faultless and blameless (Ephesians 1:4; 5:27; Philippians 1:10; Colossians 1:22; 1 Thessalonians 3:13; 5:23).

Our life on earth gains its significance from the cross of Jesus. The cross is our guiding light. It governs our life on earth. By His cross, Jesus shows our way in a dark and dangerous world. It makes sense of our strange journey from birth to death as a pilgrimage from earth to heaven. It is something like the Southern Cross for those of us who live in Australia and elsewhere in the Southern Hemisphere. This constellation of four stars is such a distinctive feature in our night sky that we have it depicted on our national flag. Its location near the two Pointers marks due south for us. So wherever we are in our land at night, we can find our location and gain direction from it. As we face that point in the night sky, due north is behind us; east is at our left side, and west is at our right side. By the Southern Cross, I locate my body on earth and in the universe. It also reminds me that Jesus is the Lamb of God, who has been crucified for me. It tells me that He now takes away the sin of the world. That includes the sins that I and everyone else have committed as well as the sins that have been committed against us. His cross helps me distinguish my shame from my guilt and frees me from them both. So, just as our life in Australia is lived under the Southern Cross, so our life in Christ is lived under His cross.

Questions for Reflection and Discussion

1. Is there anything in this chapter that you would like to discuss?

2. How did Jesus experience the full extent of human shame in His life on earth?

3. What was so shameful about His trial and crucifixion?

4. How does Jesus deliver us from shame by what He suffered for us?

5. What is our "cross"? What does Jesus call us to do by taking it up daily and following Him?

6. Why does Jesus warn His disciples that they should not be ashamed of His "Word"? (See Luke 9:26.)

CHAPTER SIX

A Sanctuary from Shame

Whoever believes in Him
will not be put to shame.

(1 Peter 2:6)

We Christians are, as Peter reminds us in his first letter, aliens in a world that is alienated from God (2:11). We live as a counter-cultural, religious community in a world that is dominated by an irreligious majority that regards us as a threat to its belief in its own spiritual autonomy and the way of life that rests on it. Despite its apparent power, it is an insecure way of life that does not and cannot deliver what it promises to provide. To counter its own insecurity, it uses shame to enforce social assimilation and reinforce conformity to its values.

Even though we live in that world, we now no longer belong to it. By His blood, Jesus has ransomed us from that futile way of life, a way of life that turns our disappointed desires into shameful passions, such as lust and greed, envy and malice, anger and hatred, and then uses them to manipulate and enslave us (1 Peter 1:18–19). We have been freed from that counterproductive lifestyle. We have been purified and sanctified by the precious blood of Jesus and

His regenerative Word, which has brought us into a holy, heavenly community here on earth (1:15–16, 22–23).

In that community, God the Father provides us with a sanctuary from shame, a place of refuge from a world that tries to shame us into submission when we refuse to toe the line and accept its terms of approval for us. This is how Peter describes that amazing safe place for us in 2:4–7a:

> [4]As you come[83] to Him [Jesus], a living stone rejected by men but in the sight of God chosen and highly honored,[84] [5]you yourselves like living stones are being built up[85] as a spiritual house,[86] to be a holy priesthood, to offer spiritual sacrifices acceptable[87] to God through Jesus Christ. [6]For it stands in the Scriptures:
>
> > "Behold, I am laying in Zion a stone,
> > a cornerstone chosen and precious,
> > and whoever believes in Him will not be put to shame."
>
> [7]So the honor is for you who believe.

Our place of refuge is the Divine Service in the new temple, the new house of God that stands in Zion, the new city of God. There, the risen Lord Jesus is our sanctuary, our place of safety from our spiritual enemies who attack our faith in Jesus, our hope in God, and our love for one another (1 Peter 1:3–7, 20–22).

---

83 Peter uses the Greek verb προσέρχομαι, which is used also in Hebrews 4:16; 7:25; 10:1, 22; 11:6; 12:18, 22. It is a liturgical term for approaching Jesus as He is present in the Divine Service.

84 ESV "precious." This is my translation. The Greek adjective here describes Jesus as both precious and highly honored.

85 This Greek verb refers to building a house as a home for people to live in and a temple for God to live in.

86 The use of "spiritual" to describe God's house and the sacrifices offered in it means that since they have to do with the Holy Spirit, they differ from the material temple and its material sacrifices in the old covenant.

87 The Greek term is more correctly translated as "well pleasing."

Here Peter recalls God's amazing promise to the citizens of Jerusalem in Isaiah 28:16, when both the city and the temple were threatened with destruction by the Assyrians. Peter envisages his hearers as a new temple as well as its new priesthood who serve God in the Divine Service. There, we come to Jesus, the living cornerstone of the new temple, so that He can make us living stones and build us up together with Him and one another as God's house. There, we are also built up as a holy priesthood to present ourselves and our money, our prayers and our praises as sacrifices that are produced by the Holy Spirit and well-pleasing to God, because they are offered through Jesus as our great High Priest and together with Him. Best of all, there in the Divine Service, Jesus make Himself available as a sanctuary from shame to those who believe in Him. There, He fulfills God's promise to His people in Isaiah 28:16 that "whoever believes in Him will not be put to shame" (author's translation). In what follows, I want to explore how God deals with our shame in each main part of the Divine Service and in the service as a whole.

The Invocation

The name of the Lord is a strong tower;
the righteous man runs into it and is safe.

(Proverbs 18:10)

The service does not begin with us and our status as children of Adam but with the triune God and His status as our God. His most holy name has been given to us as our greatest treasure in Baptism with our adoption as children of God. There, the triune God freed us from our guilt and shame as children of Adam. Through Baptism, we now have the same honored status as Jesus, the only-begotten Son of the Father, so that together with Him we can call on His heavenly Father as our Father. Through Jesus, we now have access to God the Father (Ephesians 2:18).

Our warrant for this comes from God's promise to His people in Joel 2:32 that "everyone who calls on the name of the LORD shall be saved." That bright promise was given to the citizens of Jerusalem against a dark backdrop. Since God's people had been unfaithful to Him, God unleashed a huge locust plague on the land in four stages to bring them back to Him in repentance. The devastation from the locusts led the pagan nations to shame Judah and their God with taunts, reproaches that the Lord was an absent, useless God who could do nothing to help His people (2:17). In response, God dealt with their shame in two ways with two promises. On the one hand, He promised that He would vindicate them by restoring their prosperity and would ensure that they would "never again be put to shame" (2:26–27). On the other hand, He also promised that in the last days, He will pour out His Spirit on all the people who called on the name of the Lord and will deliver them from destruction well before the great final day of judgment for the whole world.

Those promises were fulfilled in two ways. First, at Pentecost, God poured out His Holy Spirit on the disciples of Jesus and all those who were baptized in the name of Jesus Christ, so that they could call on Him for their deliverance from guilt and shame (Acts 2:14–40). Second, in Romans 10:8–17, Paul teaches that through the proclamation of the Gospel by pastors in the Divine Service, those who hear it will believe in Jesus, call on Him by name, be saved, and never again be put to shame. They will have the Lord Jesus as their refuge from shame.

That promise of deliverance from shame by Jesus is highlighted by the sentence from 1 John 1:8–9 that follows the Invocation in the first two Divine Service settings in *Lutheran Service Book*.[88] It declares that since God is faithful, He will forgive our sins; since He is just, He will cleanse us from all unrighteousness. While the Greek word for "unrighteousness" primarily means our own unrighteousness, it can also refer to the injustice that has been done to us, the abuse that we have suffered. This sentence then invites us to seek cleansing from shame as well as pardon from sin.

The Absolution

There is therefore now no condemnation
for those who are in Christ Jesus.

(Romans 8:1)

Guilt and shame are so closely entwined that it is often hard to separate them. God therefore distinguishes between them in order to deal appropriately with them both in the Divine Service. He does that in the rite of Confession and Absolution, where we receive His pardon for sin in anticipation of the last judgment. This rite comes first because it deals with the shame from sin that we feel before God, so that He can then free us from the shame that we feel from the abuse, censure, and disapproval of the people around us. The Absolution therefore distinguishes God's disapproval of sin from

88 See *LSB*, pp. 151, 167.

His approval of us. By it, He justifies the sinner without justifying the sins the sinner has committed or the sins that have been committed against the person.

An instance of this is the story of the woman caught in adultery (John 8:1–11). She had not only sinned with a man who was not her husband and been led into sin by him,[89] but she had also been publicly shamed by a group of self-righteous scribes and Pharisees who had caught her in the act of adultery and brought her to Jesus. Jesus assures her that He does not condemn her before He tells her to go and sin no more. She goes on her way guiltless and blameless before God, just as we do after the Absolution.

The Kyrie and Gloria in Excelsis

And an angel of the Lord appeared to them, and the glory of the Lord shone around them.

(Luke 2:9)

Shame gets us to focus on ourselves and our own uncertain worth rather than on God and His certain worth. So, after the Absolution, the service brings us to Jesus, who came down from heaven to earth to sacrifice Himself for us, so that through Him we could have access to God's mercy and glory in the Divine Service. First, we approach Him as needy beggars together with all other needy people who have nothing to offer Him except their spiritual poverty. Like beggars in the ancient world, we cry, "Lord, have mercy!"[90] Then we hear the song of the angels, who invite us to join

89 In Leviticus 20:10 and Deuteronomy 22:22–24, it was decreed that both the man and the woman were to be put to death. But in John 8:1–11, only the woman was singled out for condemnation.

90 See Mark 10:47–48.

them as they sing the same song that they sang for the shepherds at the birth of Jesus (Luke 2:14): "Glory to God in the highest, and on earth peace among those with whom He is pleased!" We therefore join the angels in their song of adoration for God's glory, which was revealed to people on earth through the human life of His Son and praise for the peace that Jesus offers to the people who gain God's approval through Him. After that, we add our own grateful song of praise to God the Father for His glory and to Jesus, His only Son, for taking away the sin of the world to bring peace from heaven to earth. As we praise Him for taking away the sin of the world, we also ask Him to have mercy on us and all people on earth. We therefore come into God's presence as poor beggars who have nothing to offer except our poverty and rich praise, as singers who have all that we need at our disposal because God is our heavenly Father and His Son is our human brother.

Well, what does this do for us in our shame? We secure a new status and a new sense of worth through our association with Jesus, like a poor woman who marries a rich husband. This has three parts to it in the Divine Service that together override our shame. First, we have a heavenly identity through Jesus. He makes us members of God's royal family. His Father is our Father. He gives us access to heaven here on earth. Second, we have that royal status as beggars who can call on Him in prayer for all that we need for ourselves and others in our life on earth. We can do that confidently and boldly because we know that He is pleased with us for our reliance on His Son. Third, even though we never cease to be beggars, we also stand before God together with the angels and join them in their ceaseless adoration of God the Father, Son, and Holy Spirit. We therefore have the same status as the angels—and even more than that, because we share in Christ's holiness as the only man who is holy. We therefore borrow our high status and supreme worth from Jesus. His glory covers our shame.

The Readings and the Sermon

Uphold me according to Your promise,
that I may live, and let me not be put to shame in my hope!

(Psalm 119:116)

When we have been shamed, we usually avoid people who, we fear, may shame us further with painful words and acts that threaten our fragile self-esteem. In self-defense, we become reclusive. That is especially so if someone in the church has belittled us in some way. That's why some people stay away from church and switch off when they are confronted with God's Word. To be fair, there is much in the Bible that, on face value, triggers that fear, what with all its talk about sin and God's judgment as well as His Law with all its demands and threats of punishment. When we have been shamed, we expect disapproval from others too, not just from those who have disparaged us. Even worse than that, the devil, the arch-slanderer, makes sure that we mistake God's disapproval of sin as His disapproval of us as sinners and victims of sin. He convinces us that we are so bad that God could not ever accept us or approve of us.

When we come to church, we do, indeed, come into the presence of God, the Judge of all (Hebrews 12:23). But He is a judge unlike any other judge, because He is concerned with our conscience. Like a doctor, He assesses our spiritual state in order to diagnose our sickness and heal us. He distinguishes between our guilt from the wrongs that we have done and our shame from the wrongs that have been done to us. He exposes our guilt in order to pardon us and our shame in order to deliver us from it. Both imperil our spiritual health. Since they work with each other to infect us, they are all too easily confused. But they are not the same. Each has its own cause and its own cure.

Jesus treats us through the Holy Word that is read and proclaimed to us in the Divine Service. His words are healthy, healing words (1 Timothy 6:3; 2 Timothy 1:13), words that give "sound doctrine" or healthy teaching that heals because they rightly distinguish between God's Law and His Gospel (1 Timothy 1:10; 2 Timothy 4:3; Titus 1:9; 2:1). Through His healing words, Jesus heals our conscience. By His use of God's Law, Jesus shows us that we who have done wrong need to seek God's pardon for our guilt, and we who have been wronged need to seek God's deliverance from our shame. By His use of God's Gospel, Jesus justifies repentant sinners and vindicates the self-confessed victims of sin.

Hebrews 4:12–13 explains how God uses His spoken Word to heal us and give us a place of rest for our souls in the Divine Service:

> [12]For the word of God is living and active, sharper than any two-edged sword,[91] piercing to the division of soul and spirit,

---

91 Where this noun usually refers to an arm-length sword, it can also be used to describe a much shorter knife.

of joints and of marrow, and discerning the thoughts and intentions of the heart. [13]And no creature is hidden from His sight, but all are naked and exposed to the eyes of Him to whom we must give account.

God is like a skilled surgeon who performs an operation to save the life of a cancer-ridden person. He does not operate on the body but on the soul and spirit. He does not use an X-ray to discover what is hidden from the naked eye but uses His piercing Law to diagnose the location and extent of the tumors. Then He uses His life-giving, lifesaving Gospel, rather than a sharp scalpel, to remove the cancerous sin from the soul, and He medicates the infected spirit. By means of the Gospel, He justifies penitent sinners and vindicates the self-confessed victims of sin.

Since healing from guilt and shame comes from the proclamation of God's Word as Law and Gospel, the devil does his level best to keep us from attending the Divine Service. As is shown by his name, he slanders not just us, so that we feel that we are so bad that we can't be healed, but also Jesus as a quack doctor who can't heal us with His "worthless" Word, the Word of the cross, the Word of life and health through His shameful death to atone for sin. Satan uses the people around us to make us feel ashamed of Jesus and what He promises to do for us with His Word. Then we feel too ashamed to admit that we are unwell and need to undergo treatment by our doctor. And so we go into a state of spiritual denial. We silence the voice of our conscience and pretend that all is well with us.

In Romans 1:16–17, Paul tackles our natural human embarrassment at the shameful message that he preached, the offensive message of redemption by Jesus as the crucified Messiah, with this proud avowal:[92]

> [16]I am not ashamed of the gospel, for it is the power of God for salvation to everyone who believes, to the Jew first and also to the Greek.
>
> [17]For in it the righteousness of God is revealed from faith for faith, as it is written, "The righteous shall live by faith."[93]

Paul asserts that the message that seems to add shame to shame in fact liberates from the worst shame, the shame of God's present disapproval and final condemnation—and that for four reasons. First, it is the Gospel of God, the good news of salvation from guilt and shame for all people rather than just for the Jews. Second, it is not just the Good News of salvation for us at the end of the world but is also a powerful message by which God Himself saves us from sin, death, and the devil already now as it is preached. It does what is says. It frees guilty people from sin and abused people from shame. Third, by the proclamation of the Gospel, God the Judge "reveals" His righteousness to all people by justifying those who have sinned and vindicating those who are victims of human injustice. This revelation, this apocalypse, banishes the fear of God's rejection because it anticipates God's final verdict and sentence at the Last Judgment. Fourth, deliverance is given as a free gift to everyone who believes in Jesus and the Good News He proclaims.

---

92 For a similar avowal of freedom from shame, see 2 Timothy 1:12.

93 See Habakkuk 2:4.

The faith that receives God's deliverance and enjoys eternal life rests entirely on the proclamation of the Gospel from its beginning to its end, from its origin to its completion. Those who believe in the Gospel travel with Jesus on a journey that leads further and deeper into a guilt-free, shame-free life with God the Father.

The Creed

No one who denies the Son has the Father.
Whoever confesses the Son has the Father also.

(1 John 2:23)

Just recently, my wife and I watched a series on Netflix that told the story of the relationship between a singer and the woman that he loved. She had been shamed by her former partner, who had belittled her as a woman and the mother of his child. By his rejection of her, he silenced her as his partner. In contrast with her experience with her former partner, she admitted to the singer, "With you I really am myself." Her confidence in him and his outspoken affirmation of her lifted her shame and restored her sense of worth. That was evident in their open conversation and easy agreement with each other.

Jesus does that and much more with us. Through His Word, He shows who He really is and who we really are. By His words of justification and approval, He gives us confidence in Him and His concern for us. He puts us at ease with Him. We, in turn, open up to Him because He is open with us. We lose our diffidence, with its fear of rejection, and openly confess our faith in Him. With Him, we are at last as we were meant to be. We have no need to hide in shame but gladly express our confidence in Him as our Lord. We say a wholehearted yes to Him and all that He has done for us. We have freedom of speech with Him.

In his letter to the Romans, Paul recalls God's assurance to His people in Deuteronomy 30:14 about the ongoing impact of His indwelling Word on them and uses it to describe how God frees us from shame by our confession of faith in Jesus as our Lord:

> [6]The righteousness based on faith says, . . . [8]"The word is near you, in your mouth and in your heart" (that is, the word of faith that we proclaim); [9]because, if you confess with your mouth that Jesus is Lord and believe in your heart that God raised Him from the dead, you will be saved. [10]For with the heart one believes and is justified, and with the mouth one confesses and is saved. [11]For the Scripture says, "Everyone who believes in Him will not be put to shame." (Romans 10:6, 8–11)

Our Lord Jesus speaks the embodied Word of righteousness, the message of justification and vindication to us through His preachers in the Divine Service. The Word opens our hearts to believe in Jesus and receive God's pardon and approval through faith in Him. It also opens our lips to confess our common faith in Jesus with one another before God. Through faith in the death and resurrection of Jesus for us, we are saved from shame, the shame that we have from our wrongdoings and wrongs that have been done to us. As we confess our common faith in the triune God, the Word that vindicates us becomes part of us. It is on our lips because it is in our hearts. The Word that Jesus speaks to us in our hearts and is spoken to us through the people in our congregation frees us inwardly and outwardly from shame and assures us that we will never be put to shame as long as we believe in Jesus. We have supernatural affirmation and validation. As we confess Jesus as God's Son to the people around us, Jesus confesses us as His siblings before His Father and the angels in heaven (Matthew 10:32; Luke 12:8). Since we believe in the triune God and are not ashamed to call Him our God, He is not ashamed to be called our God (Hebrews 11:16).

The Prayer of the Church

> We do not have a high priest who is unable to sympathize
> with our weaknesses, but one who in every respect
> has been tempted as we are, yet without sin. Let us then
> with confidence draw near to the throne of grace, that we may
> receive mercy and find grace to help in time of need.
>
> (Hebrews 4:15–16)

When people are badly shamed, they lose their voice. When Christians are shamed and made to feel ashamed of themselves, they find it hard to pray for themselves as they should and to ask God to deliver them from their shame. Yet He is the only one who can free them from shame and the complex fallout from it. It gets even harder than that because they know that Jesus tells them to pray for those who abuse them emotionally and physically (Luke 6:27–28) and who persecute them for their faith in Jesus (Matthew 5:44–45;

see also 5:10–11). After all, that is what Jesus did for those who crucified Him. And that's what He does for us as our High Priest when we are abused. He intercedes for us in our weakness, so that we can join Him in praying for mercy for ourselves and others like us.

It is true that people in many religions value prayer. When they are in trouble and don't know where else to turn for help, they pray to their gods or ask their religious leaders to intercede for them. But they usually do that for themselves, their families, and their friends rather than outsiders and strangers, let alone their enemies. They do not offer common prayer for one another and all people, both friends or enemies. Yet, in contrast to what was usually done, Paul tells Timothy (in 1 Timothy 2:1–6) that the first thing the congregation in Ephesus had to do was to pray for all people and for all their Roman rulers, including the emperor, who had already begun to persecute them. Since Jesus gave His life as a ransom for all people, He was the mediator between God and all of them. So since God wanted all people to be saved, the church was to intercede for them all. And that is what we also do in the Divine Service.

We offer many different prayers in different parts of the service. In fact, we actually offer ten sets of petitions throughout the traditional order of service.[94] They all revolve around the Prayer of the Church, which comes after the sermon as our response to God's service of us with His Word.[95] Yet, in all of these petitions, we stand together with Jesus, our great High Priest, who intercedes with His heavenly Father for us and leads us in our common prayer

94 See *LSB*, pp. 184–202.
95 See *LSB*, p. 193.

for ourselves, the whole church, the whole world, and all people in need. He helps us to do what we cannot otherwise do, disabled as we are by our guilt and shame.

We acknowledge that we all stand on common ground before God and that we all depend entirely on His mercy with the repeated cry for Jesus to have mercy on us in the Divine Service. In the ancient world, that was the usual cry for help by beggars, who said, "Lord, have mercy on me." In the Psalms, that too was the cry of needy people to God for help in trouble.[96] But in Psalm 123, it is the cry of God's people as a company of beggars for deliverance from the scorn and contempt of their enemies.[97] And that is how it is used in the Divine Service. So in the traditional order of service, it is the congregation's petition to Jesus seven times in all:[98] three times in the Kyrie, two times in the Gloria, and three times in the Agnus Dei. In all cases, the petition for mercy on "us" includes all the members of the congregation and the whole church as well as all people on earth. The extent of this plea for mercy is evident from its appeal to Jesus as the Lamb of God, who takes away the sin of the world, in the Gloria and the Agnus Dei. That appeal recalls the witness of John the Baptist to Jesus in John 1:29, where he declares, "Behold, the Lamb of God, who takes away the sin of the world!"

The common appeal for mercy is amazing for two reasons. On the one hand, in it we do not just ask Jesus to take my sins, or our sins, as we would expect, but "the sin of the world." The singular noun "sin" is immensely significant. It includes all the sins that

96 See Psalms 6:3–4; 9:13; 25:16; 26:11; 27:7; 30:10; 31:9; 41:4, 10; 51:1; 56:1; 57:1; 86:3, 16; 119:58, 132.
97 See Matthew 9:27; 20:30–31; and Luke 17:13 for the use of the plural form, "Have mercy on us."
98 See *LSB*, pp. 186, 188, 198.

all people have ever committed and will ever commit as well as all the sins that all people have ever suffered from all people who have ever abused them. We ask Jesus to have mercy on all of us, whether we have done wrong or been wronged, whether we have shamed others or been shamed by others. The only hope for any of us is His mercy. On the other hand, we can ask Him for His mercy on all of us because Jesus is the Lamb of God, the only truly innocent human victim of sin, who offered Himself as a sacrifice to remove the sin of the world. He stands with us in our guilt and shame and pleads with His heavenly Father to have mercy on us. He takes away our guilt and shame and covers us with innocence and holiness. Since we have Him as our victim and priest, we can pray in His name and together with Him for ourselves, the church, and the world with His own prayer, the Lord's Prayer, as well as in the Prayer of the Church.

The Sacrament

Blessed are those who are invited
to the marriage supper of the Lamb.

(Revelation 19:9)

We honor people by inviting them to come home to dinner with us. We single them out for even greater social honor and personal approval by inviting them to celebrate an important occasion in our lives, such as a special birthday or our wedding. We, in turn, are honored by those who accept our hospitality. They are our friends, the people we value, the people whose approval and acceptance we seek.

In the ancient world, the greatest honor that a king could show to any of his subjects was to invite them to dinner as his guests at his palace once or occasionally or—best of all—permanently. So his courtiers, his ministers of government, had permanent seats for dinner at his table in his palace, together with his son and heir and the other adult members of his royal family. His guests were regarded as honorary members of the royal family. That's the same honor that Jesus confers on His apostles at the Last Supper in Luke 22:28–30, after His institution of Holy Communion and His teaching on their rank, with this amazing declaration:

> 28You are those who have stayed with Me in My trials, 29and I assign to you, as My Father assigned to Me, a kingdom, 30that you may eat and drink at My table in My kingdom and sit on thrones judging[99] the twelve tribes of Israel.

Here, Jesus—God's Son and heir—shares His kingship with the apostles as His royal brothers. As His permanent guests, they depend on Him for their livelihood and reign over God's people together with Him.[100]

Like the apostles, we, too, are Jesus' royal guests in His Holy Supper. Even better than that, He treats us as brothers and sisters in His royal family. That honor does not depend on our social, moral, or religious standing, but on His generosity and high regard for us as God's adopted children. What greater affirmation of our worth could we have than that? In fact, He spreads His table before us in

99 As in the Old Testament, this term is used broadly for all the work of a king. Here it refers to the Office of the Keys, the ministry of Word and Sacrament.

100 For a fuller exposition of this passage, see Arthur A. Just Jr., *Luke 9:51–24:53*, Concordia Commentary (Concordia Publishing House, 1997), 847–50.

the presence of our enemies (Psalm 23:5). That includes the devil and all his cronies, who are intent on discrediting and shaming us.

In His Supper, Jesus deals with our shame in three ways. First, like the marriage of a husband with his wife, He celebrates His union with us by giving Himself to us with His body and blood. By this union—which is both personal and communal—He covers our shame and confers His own spiritual status on us as His holy Bride. As in an engagement before a marriage, He gives us a foretaste of eternal life with Him in heaven, for that is where our union with Him will be fully consummated (Revelation 19:7, 9). Second, we meet with Him in Holy Communion clothed in the robe that He has provided for us in Baptism, the robe of His righteousness and holiness, which covers our guilt and shame (Matthew 22:11–12; Revelation 19:7–8; 21:2). There, He then presents us to Himself and His Father for acceptance and admiration as His radiant, holy and blameless, unblemished and faultless Bride (Ephesians 5:27; Colossians 1:22). Third, and most wonderfully, He gives us His holy, innocent blood to drink in order to cleanse us completely from all guilt and shame. His blood is not put on our bodies to purify them, like the blood of sacrificed animals on the priest in the old covenant (Exodus 29:19–21; Leviticus 8:23–25, 30) but is put on our hearts to cleanse us entirely and make us completely holy in body, soul, and spirit (Hebrews 9:13–14; 1 Thessalonians 5:23).

The power of Christ's blood to free us from shame was shown to me some years ago when I preached a sermon on the gift of Christ's blood in Holy Communion in Malaysia. There, I mentioned that

Jesus gives us His blood to share His life, His purity, and His holiness with us. When I spoke about our purification with His blood, I recalled the declaration in 1 John 1:7–8 that the blood of Jesus cleanses us from "all sin" and "all unrighteousness" and explained that this also included cleansing from the taint of abuse, cleansing from the shame that we feel when people sin against us. I also spoke about Christ's gift of His blood for "the remission of sins," our release from them. As I was helping the pastor distribute the Lord's Supper after the sermon, I was struck by a young woman who was crying as she received the chalice from me. She was dressed in drab clothes and stayed kneeling at the altar until the end of the distribution. When the service was over, the pastor elatedly told me that something remarkable had happened. He did not have time to tell me about it there in the vestry because we needed to greet the people at the door of the church. When that woman came to us, she fell on her knees before me, took both my hands in hers, kissed them, and said, "Thank you! Thank you!"

After all the people had left, the pastor told me more about her. The last time she had communed was at her confirmation eight years earlier. But her life had been ruined soon afterward by sexual abuse from a member of her own family. No matter how much her pastors had tried to help her, they could not remove the awful taint, the crippling sense of impurity and shame from that abuse. Since then, if she did come to church, she always came in after the service had begun, sat at the back of the church, and sneaked out before the celebration of Holy Communion. But Christ's promise of remission of sins and her reliance on the blood of Jesus for cleansing changed all that. When I was next there some years later, I met her again and found out that she had married and become the mother of two children.

The Lord's Supper fulfills the hope and prayer in the psalms for a spiritual sanctuary, a safe place, a place of refuge from shame for God's people.[101] There we receive a foretaste of what we hope for from Jesus, our great High Priest, who purifies our conscience (Hebrews 9:14; 10:22) and sanctifies us with His blood (10:29; 13:12). That's why the author of Hebrews speaks about the risen, ascended Jesus as our place of refuge in 6:19–20. Jesus is our sure and certain hope. With Him and His presence with us in the Lord's Supper, we have a supernatural, heavenly sanctuary from shame here on earth.

The Benediction

Make Your face shine on Your servant;
save me in Your steadfast love!
O LORD, let me not be put to shame,
for I call upon You.

(Psalm 31:16–17)

Some years ago, I led a number of congregational workshops on the Divine Service. In the workshops, I included a questionnaire in which I listed all the main parts of the service and asked the participants to pick which of these helped them most in their journey of faith. Once they had done that, I asked each person to share

101 See Psalms 25:20; 31:1; 71:1. See also the description of the Lord as the place of refuge from all enemies in Psalms 14:6; 46:1; 61:3; 62:7, 8; 71:7; 73:28; 91:2, 9; 94:22; 142:5.

what part he or she chose, and why. One woman surprised us all by saying that it was the Benediction. When I asked her why, she said that she came to church each Sunday to receive God's blessing for the week to come, because she found it hard to cope without it. In the break after the session, I asked her to elaborate on that remark. She told me that she often felt a complete failure as a wife, a mother, a daughter, a friend, and a Christian. But that blessing assured her that Jesus approved of her and was pleased with her. So she went home with the picture of His face smiling at her as He told her how much He appreciated her, loved her, and cared for her.

Like that woman, the Israelites attended the service at the tabernacle and the temple to receive God's blessing. That was what God had promised to give them there (Exodus 20:24). There, He conveyed His blessing to them at the end of the service with the benediction that He gave to the high priest, Aaron, and his successors with this command:

> [23]Thus you shall bless the people of Israel: you shall say to them,
>
> [24] The LORD bless you and keep you;
> [25] the LORD make His face to shine upon you
> and be gracious to you;
> [26] the LORD lift up His countenance[102] upon you
> and give you peace.
>
> [27]So shall they put My name upon the people of Israel, and I will bless them. (Numbers 6:23–27)

102 His face.

This was not a prayer nor a wish but an enactment, a speech act by which God Himself actually blessed His people through the high priest. In it, God granted six of His best gifts for the life of His people on earth. And He does the same for us with the same benediction at the end of the service.

In Luke 24:50–51, Luke reports that when Jesus had completed His work on earth, He took His eleven apostles to Bethany, where He was taken from their sight into heaven as He blessed them. There, Jesus now serves us as our High Priest before His Father and conveys the Father's blessing from heaven to earth for us. Through Jesus, God the Father now blesses us with every spiritual blessing, so that we are now holy and blameless before Him (Ephesians 1:3–4).

Well, what then does the risen Lord Jesus provide for us in the Aaronic benediction? He blesses us with the gift of the Holy Spirit and protects our bodies and souls from Satan and all spiritual harm and danger; He makes His friendly face shine on us, like a parent on their dear child, and approves of us; He lifts up His smiling face in eye-to-eye contact with us to show that He is pleased with us and gives us heavenly peace in our troubled lives here on earth. As the angels announced at the birth of Jesus, God has given us His peace because He is pleased with us (Luke 2:14). Just as Jesus announces the Father's word of pardon to us to deal with our guilt at the beginning of the service, so He announces His Father's word of blessing to deal with our shame at its end so that we can be sure that we will live without shame for all eternity.

What an Honor!

The introduction to this chapter referred to Peter's assurance of our deliverance from shame through our participation in the Divine Service (1 Peter 2:4–6). He spoke to us of Jesus as the "highly honored" cornerstone of God's new temple, with us as living stones in it, and made this amazing declaration: "So the honor is for you who believe" (2:7a). Then, in 2:9–10, he explains how Jesus honors us. He declares:

> *9*But you are a chosen race,[103] a royal priesthood,[104] a holy nation,[105] a people for His own possession,[106] that you may proclaim the excellencies of Him who called you out of darkness into His marvelous light.
>
> *10*Once you were not a people, but now you are God's people; once you had not received mercy, but now you have received mercy.

What a change of status! Jesus confers four unearned honors on us who—unlike the people of Israel—were "not a people," nobodies who had no claim on God's mercy. But through our union with Jesus, we share in His divine status and worth. We who were doomed descendants of Adam are now part of God's chosen race through our rebirth in Baptism and adoption into God's family. We who were once alienated from God and excluded from His presence are now a royal priesthood as members of His royal family, who serve Him as priests together with Jesus. We who were once

103 See Deuteronomy 7:6–8; Isaiah 43:20.

104 See Exodus 19:6; Isaiah 61:6; Revelation 1:6; 5:10.

105 See Exodus 19:6; Deuteronomy 14:2; 26:19.

106 See Exodus 19:5; Deuteronomy 14:2; 26:19; Malachi 3:17; Titus 2:14.

unclean sinners are now a holy nation who share in His holiness. We who once did not belong to God are now a people of His own possession, His most cherished treasure.

Jesus therefore honors us by sharing His status with us as God's chosen Son, God's great High Priest, the Holy One of God, and His greatest treasure. He confers this honor on us as an act of mercy rather than as a reward for service by calling us from the darkness of sin and death, guilt and shame into the marvelous light of His presence in the Divine Service. He honors us greatly so that we in turn may proclaim His excellence to the world around us. What better way could there be for Him to free us from shame than that!

Questions for Reflection and Discussion

1. Is there anything in this chapter that you would like to discuss?

2. Where and how is Jesus our sanctuary from shame?

3. What do you find surprising in all the different ways that God delivers us from shame in the Divine Service? What do these ways have in common?

4. Which part of the service is most helpful for you in dealing with the shame that you have experienced?

5. How does Jesus honor those who believe in Him?

6. How does the devil use our shame to keep us away from church? Why?

CHAPTER SEVEN

Gracious Speech

But now you must put them all away:
anger, wrath, malice, slander,[107]
and shameful[108] speech from your mouth.

(Colossians 3:8, author's translation)

Words matter much more than we realize. That is especially so if they are spoken directly to us. They make or break us because they establish our social standing and confirm our public reputation. Our public standing depends on them. Our personal self-esteem, our sense of worth, is determined by them.

While the words of others can defame and shame us, they can also affirm and honor us. They put us down and lift us up; they wound us and heal us; they help us and harm us; they put us to death and give us life. While Satan turns them into weapons in a war of words,[109] the Holy Spirit uses them to make peace. At its worst, a tongue that has been set alight by hell can kindle a fire that damages the whole life of a soul, like a little spark that kindles

107 The Greek word here is βλασφημία, "blasphemy," which describes abusive speech that slanders a person or God.

108 My literal translation. The ESV takes this phrase more narrowly as a reference to obscene speech.

109 This graphic term comes from 1 Timothy 6:3–5, where Paul warns against ungodly, doctrinal "word warfare" that produces "envy, dissension, slander, evil suspicions, and constant friction," because it disagrees with "the sound words of our Lord Jesus Christ." See also 2 Timothy 2:14.

a bush fire that burns a whole forest (James 3:5–6). It is therefore true that "death and life are in the power of the tongue" (Proverbs 18:21).

The power of the spoken word is shown most clearly and vividly in a court of law. The social standing of a person is determined for better or worse by what is said in a trial. There, the defendant pleads guilty or not guilty after being charged with an offense. There, the counsel for the prosecution presents the case against the defendant, while the counsel for the defense presents the case for the innocence of the defendant. The case for or against the defendant rests on the verbal testimony of eyewitnesses and the truth of what they say. The whole trial is governed by a judge who eventually delivers the verdict and the sentence. All this is done with words that either convict or vindicate the person on trial.

Since our self-esteem is influenced by the approval or disapproval of others in our social setting, we are at their mercy for the affirmation and confirmation of our personal honor. What they say to us and about us confers and confirms our standing with them, our status in our families and communities. We are, as it were, in a continuous trial in the court of public opinion. This court, however, has no judge to ensure proper procedure and a just outcome. The people around us either enhance or belittle our reputation by whether they bear true witness to us or false witness against us. In the absence of a proper judge, they also function as a kind of jury that passes its judgment on us by the opinion of the majority rather than the law. By their judgment, they either befriend us or unfriend us.

Poisonous Speech

Since our self-esteem and sense of worth depends mostly, if not entirely, on how others regard us and what they say of us, we are easily shamed. We are severely shamed by what is now rather crudely and fashionably called "hate speech," speech that is meant to disparage and discredit us. It does not just censure us for the bad things that we have done or even our wrong opinions; it also asserts that we are bad, wicked, worthless people. In Colossians 3:8, Paul calls it "shameful speech" (author's translation)—speech that maliciously intends to shame us.

We Christians are beset by shame speech on two fronts: verbal abuse from the world around us and unkind words from people in the church. So, on the one hand, Jesus warns us that since we are His disciples, we will be falsely reviled and maligned, publicly hated and rejected because of our allegiance to Him (Matthew 5:11; Luke 6:22). He also encourages us to counter hateful speech with the practice of love for the speakers (Luke 6:27–28). We are to bless them[110] when they curse us and pray for them when they abuse us. Paradoxically, their verbal abuse of us discloses their unacknowledged need for God's grace; it is an unconscious cry from their hearts for God's pardon, approval, and love as well as a call from God for us to pray for them and bless them. Inspired by these words of Jesus, Paul also encourages us to practice positive

110 The literal sense of the Greek verb εὐλογέω is to "speak well" of someone. That is done in many ways, ranging from flattery to a polite greeting that wishes someone well, like "Stay safe!" and a word of thanks for a gift, to a spoken compliment, like "Well done!" and outspoken praise. The opposite of "blessing" people is speaking badly of them and speaking something bad against them by cursing them with words that "wish" something bad will happen to them or, even, that they will die and end up in hell.

retaliation by blessing those who curse us (Romans 12:14, 17, 21). Likewise, in 1 Peter 3:9–16, we are urged to speak well of those who revile us for our good behavior and bless them by our respectful, gentle, hopeful confession of faith in Jesus. Then they, rather than we, will be put to shame when they slander us (3:16), while we will have no reason to be ashamed by their insults because we will be richly blessed by the Holy Spirit, who rests on us and glorifies us (4:14–16).

As well as this, we also face verbal disparagement from people in the church. That is far worse than from unbelievers. It hurts more and does greater damage because it calls into question our spiritual status and identity as holy children of God. It hits us harder because we are far from morally blameless and spiritually irreproachable. So in what follows, I want to tackle that difficult issue as best I can. Two spiritual truths help us to deal with shaming speech from our fellow Christians: the truth that our status and worth is not achieved by us but ascribed to us by God the Father though our union with Jesus and our faith in Him, and the truth that the devil is a slanderer who is set on discounting our spiritual status as children of the heavenly Father by destroying our faith in Him and His Word. Most perniciously, the devil uses us to censure, slander, and shame one another, so that we get caught up in an ongoing, escalating cycle of verbal character assassination.

That attack usually begins in secret when we fall out with our brothers and sisters in Christ. We think badly of them and dwell on their real or imagined slights against us and other people. Then we set the cycle of disparagement in motion by spreading gossip about them to our friends and like-minded hearers (Romans 1:29; 2 Corinthians 12:20). We misrepresent them and present them in a bad light. By our secret censure of them, we undermine their reputation and arouse suspicion of them. Then we openly tell lies about them to others, lies that range from things that are half true to quite false (Ephesians 4:25; Colossians 3:9). That culminates in outright slander against our fellow believers (Matthew 15:19; 2 Corinthians 12:20; Ephesians 4:31; Colossians 3:8; 1 Timothy 6:4; James 4:11; 1 Peter 2:1). We do not just slander the people who have slighted us; we, in turn, actually become slanderers (Romans 3:5–8; 1 Corinthians 4:9–13). And that unleashes a further cycle of verbal abuse. Those whom we have shamed by what we have said retaliate by disparaging and shaming us.

The slander that occurs in the church is often more subtle and discreet than that in the world. We do not just censure the wrong things that people have said or done; we denigrate them personally and discredit them spiritually as immoral, unrighteous, and unholy people. Let me illustrate this from my own experience. I have been called a "bully" because I have privately rebuked fellow pastors for their misbehavior; I have been called an "intolerant fanatic" because I disapprove of same-sex marriage; I have been called "a narrow-minded bigot" because I hold that God has created each person as either male or female; I have been called a "woman-hater" because I reject the ordination of women; I have been called a "heretic" because I teach that the headship of a husband over his wife mirrors the headship of Jesus over the church as His dear Bride. It is telling that all these slurs have to do with the divergence of Christian doctrine from fashionable secular dogmas. By attacking me, the attackers all, in some way, also indirectly and unintentionally discredit Jesus and disregard what He says. They try to silence me by shaming me, so that I no longer confess the whole truth of God.

Ending the Cycle

In his letters to both the Ephesians and the Colossians, Paul describes the cycle of hate speech and tells us what God does to arrest and reverse it. This cycle usually begins with lies that have been told about us (Ephesians 4:25; Colossians 3:9), lies that have hurt and shamed and embittered us (Ephesians 4:31). We then react to these lies with anger at what has been said about us and rage against those who have slighted us (Ephesians 4:31; Colossians 3:8). Anger, unless it is checked, opens our hearts to the devil, the slanderer (Ephesians 4:26–27). He gets us to brood over the slight that we have experienced and replay it over and over again in our imagination from day to day. He stokes up our anger by reminding us of all the other bad things the offender has ever said and done.[111] That easily justified rage at our unjust treatment breeds malice in thought, word, and deed. In self-defense, we retaliate, openly and publicly, with an outburst of verbal abuse and slander against the offender (Ephesians 4:31). So hate speech usually produces hate speech; angry shame speech all too readily incites even worse malicious shame speech.

---

111 The destructive effect of anger has been confirmed by medical research, which has discovered that anger damages our physical and mental health. It harms our hearts, brains, and gastrointestinal system and does even greater damage to our whole lives than anxiety and sadness do.

This vicious cycle of verbal abuse is broken by our adoption as God's children in Baptism. There, Jesus puts to death our old shame-full, sin-damaged self and gives us a new self that is "created after the likeness of God in true righteousness and holiness" (Ephesians 4:24). He takes on our shame and remakes us in His image. We therefore share in His status and worth as God's Son. In God's sight, we are as righteous and holy and free from shame as Jesus is. Thus when God the Father considers us, He no longer sees us as we once were, but as we now are in Jesus. He honors and affirms each of us with the same words that He spoke to Jesus at His Baptism: "You are My beloved son; you are My beloved daughter; with you I am well pleased" (Mark 1:11, adapted). And that has far-reaching consequences for us. It creates a new way of life for us that is marked by five changes.

First, God the Father gives us His Holy Spirit to re-create us as new people and make us like Him in His righteousness and holiness (Ephesians 4:24). He re-creates us in Jesus, whom He has anointed with His Holy Spirit, to reign together with Jesus in God's kingdom by administering His grace on earth (2:6–7, 10). He does not just reign over us; He reigns in us and through us. We therefore do not just work for Him but also work with Him. He does His work through us. This is how Luther describes this in a sermon for Pentecost based on John 14:23–31:

> This is how it goes: beyond the grace by which a person begins to believe and holds to the Word, God also rules in the person through His divine power and activity. . . . Such a person also grows and progresses daily in life and good works

> and becomes a kind, gentle and patient person . . . a person through whom God speaks, lives and works. Such a person's tongue is God's tongue, such a person's hand is God's hand, such a person's word is no longer a human word, but God's Word. (WA 21:458–59)

Second, Jesus replaces our old self, our old identity, the humanity that we have inherited from Adam, with a new self, a new identity, the humanity that we receive from Jesus (Ephesians 4:22–24). So now we no longer gain our status and worth from other people but from God as His free gift to us. We get a new "Christian" identity, a Christian name, from Him rather than from our parents or ancestors or anybody else. It is not achieved by us with our own efforts but is ascribed to us as our inalienable inheritance from God through Baptism. Like orphans who have been adopted, we have a new name, a new identity, a new status, and a new way of life in a new family. In fact, we live in a new world without leaving the world that we entered at our human birth.

Third, even though we may rightly value the approval and recognition of the people around us, we do not need to justify ourselves to them by what we do or say and how we live. We are justified by God as our Creator and Judge. We therefore depend on Him and His Word for our personal status and sense of worth. By our union with Jesus and our faith in Him, we have His heavenly Father's pardon and approval. Our honor and freedom from shame depend on Him.

Fourth, Jesus frees us from the vicious cycle of shame speech. He Himself endured the worst of it for us with His unjust trial and His shameful death on the cross; He now offers to shoulder it for us. Thus, in Ephesians 4:31, Paul says to each of us, "Let all bitterness and wrath and anger and clamor and slander be put away from you, along with all malice."[112] Not some of it, but all of it! He knows that we can't get rid of it by ourselves. That's why he uses a passive imperative to tell us what God wants to do for us. He says, "Let it be put away! Let it be taken away! Let it be removed!" He urges us to let it all go and let Jesus remove it from us with His Holy Spirit. We do that by faith by handing it all over to Him in prayer and asking Him to fix it for us. The picture that Paul uses is of us undressing from dirty clothing with an unexpected twist. We do not undress ourselves; God undresses us in order to dress us up with a brand-new set of beautiful clothes, clothes that we borrow from Jesus.[113]

Fifth, through the Holy Spirit, whom Jesus has given to show us that we belong to Him,[114] we ask Jesus to "put off" the trappings that belong to our old self, like the set of old, dirty clothes at the end of a day before we go to bed, and "put on" or dress us up us with the right behavior that matches our new selves as God's holy,

---

112 Malice is the desire to harm someone. A malicious person not only wishes to inflict evil on another person by words and deeds but often delights in harming that person for what he has done. For other references to malice, see Romans 1:29; 1 Corinthians 5:8; Colossians 3:8; Titus 3:3; 1 Peter 2:1.

113 See Ephesians 4:20–24 and Colossians 3:8–14.

114 Paul uses a graphic illustration to depict this in Ephesians 4:30. He compares the gift of the Holy Spirit to a seal with the person's name or the first letter for it inscribed on it. That seal was stamped on a letter or object to show who owned it. That seal was the Greek letter *CH*, which was an abbreviation for Christ and looked like a cross. It was traced and still is traced on the forehead of a person in Baptism to show that the one who is baptized belongs to Jesus, because He purchased him or her by His death on the cross.

chosen beloved people, like a set of new, clean clothes at the beginning of a new day (Colossians 3:12–13).

Gracious Speech

Jesus does not just want to end the harmful cycle of shame speech for us; He wants us to join Him in reversing it with three counter-cultural ways of speaking.

First, inspired by Christ's instruction to seek reconciliation with those who have offended us (Matthew 18:15) as well as those who have been offended by us (5:23–26), Paul instructs us to be "speaking the truth in love" (Ephesians 4:15, 25). We should not pretend that all is well when it is not at all well; nor should we gloss over our hurt from the slights that we have experienced and the anger we feel from them. Rather, we are called to deal openly and honestly with those who have been caught up with us in the fallout from abuse. Our common membership in Christ's Body requires us to speak truthfully to one another, because what has damaged one part of the body affects the whole of it (4:25). We are called to clear the air with four kinds of truthful speech that avoid shaming one another and unleashing a new cycle of recrimination and self-justification.

If a brother or sister in Christ is angry with us, we can confront that person respectfully in private and ask the person why he or she is so upset by us. Then once the person has voiced the grievance against us, we can apologize for it and ask the person to pardon us. If a fellow Christian has enraged us by what he or she has said and done, we can also confront that person in private and tell how he or she has hurt us, speaking humbly and respectfully, as one offender with another offender. The person then can apologize for the words or deeds and ask for our pardon, if and when he or she is moved to do so by Christ and His Spirit. Incidentally, this kind of truth speaking also clears up misinformation and misunderstanding. It promotes warm, honest, and unfeigned transparency. It removes the need for concealment for fear of retribution and serves to maintain the reputation of both parties.

Second, Paul urges us to step down from our self-righteous high horses and engage in grace-speech with one another (Ephesians 4:32–5:2).[115] He says:

> [32]Be kind to one another, tenderhearted, gracious to one another as God in Christ was gracious to you. [5:1]Therefore be imitators of God, as beloved children. [2]And walk in love, as Christ loved us and gave Himself for us, a fragrant offering and sacrifice to God.

The language here is warm and affectionate. It is not the cold idiom of a court of law but the heartfelt language of love, the love of a happily married couple for each other or the love of a mother for her troubled child. Since God the Father has dealt so graciously with us, His dear rebellious children, by sacrificing His Son for us, we can be kind and tenderhearted with those who have hurt and angered us.[116] We can speak warmly and graciously to those

115 See also Colossians 3:12–13. This is my translation. Paul uses a verb that is derived from the Greek word for "grace." While it can refer to forgiveness, which is how it is usually translated, it is also used more broadly elsewhere to describe the generous bestowal of other gifts as well (see Luke 7:21; Romans 8:32; Philippians 2:9; 1 Corinthians 2:12).

116 In Colossians 3:12–13, Paul associates being gracious with "patience" and "bearing with" others. The

who have spoken maliciously about us and to us. As people who have experienced God's grace, we can now offer the same kind of grace and favor, pardon and acceptance, approval and generosity to those who have hurt us. We can give of ourselves in love by what we say to them, and how.

Third, Paul tells us how to do this in Ephesians 4:29. He says:

> Let no corrupting talk come out of your mouths, but only such as is good for building up, as fits the occasion, that it may give grace to those who hear.

Paul here compares shame speech with something rotten, putrid, and disgusting, like bad food that is vomited up to prevent it from poisoning the body. It does not infect just the speaker but also the whole community. We are all nourished by God's wholesome words of grace. So since we have been reclaimed by Jesus and sealed with His Holy Spirit, we can respond to shame speech with grace speech. We can speak words of grace that do not punish but pardon, kind words that do not poison but nourish, soft words that do not hurt but heal, gentle words that do not denigrate but appreciate, respectful words that do not antagonize but conciliate. This kind of speech is qualified in two ways. On the one hand, it speaks good words that are fit for the situation and occasion. They do not follow a set agenda but respond to each person in each situation. Before they are spoken, the speaker pays attention to the whole situation and listens to what is said. Then and only then does he respond with due consideration by saying what needs to be said.

Greek word for "patience" means "long-temperedness," the opposite of being short-tempered with those who offend us. Similarly, when we "bear with" others, we do not merely tolerate them, but we hold ourselves back from hasty reaction or overreaction to what they have said or done. Here and in Ephesians 4:2, it may then refer to holding our tongues in love for them.

On the other hand, the purpose of these words is to build up rather than tear down.

The picture here is that the congregation is a house that God has built for Himself on Jesus, and each member is a stone, a building block, in it. The congregation is not a human house but is God's holy house, His temple, the place where He resides and interacts with its members, a holy place that God builds for Himself to meet with people and bless them (Ephesians 2:19–22). The words of grace that are spoken are meant to build it up and keep it holy. The congregation is also the Body of Christ, with each person a living member in it (4:15–16, 25). In that case, all the members of the Body are built up together and build themselves up in it by working together with Jesus in His mission here on earth. So, as God's holy temple and Christ's holy Body, we are all called to speak words of grace that build up the whole congregation and each person in it.

Salty Speech

In our society, Paul's call to engage in gracious speech is all too easily mistaken as an implication that we must avoid confrontation and tolerate wrongdoing. We all too readily confuse graciousness with niceness and equate constructive speech with smooth flattery. But Paul does not advocate that at all. Thus, in Colossians 4:6, he gives this advice: "Let your speech always be gracious, seasoned with salt, so that you may know how you ought to answer each person." Gracious speech is not insipid and sugary; it is salty and sharp. It does not spread infection and sickness, but fosters proper nourishment and good health. It confronts what is shameful and deals constructively with it.

In my introduction, I noted that some of my Aboriginal students used to admonish their peers when they were about to bring shame on themselves by whispering "Shame job!" as a discreet warning to them. They appealed to their sense of shame to avoid worse shame. They "shamed" them privately to prevent them from being shamed publicly. They showed how respectful shaming is beneficial and desirable.

Like guilt, our sense of shame at our shortcomings is a good gift from God that is very useful if it is not abused or misused. It has to do with our identity as people created by God in His image and likeness for life together with one another and Him. Our true identity is not something that we acquire or construct for ourselves; it is ascribed to us and conferred on us by our Creator. It is not just a matter of our self-esteem and self-worth, but it is the honor and respect that we have from God as men and women who have been made in His image to represent and reflect Him. We therefore feel ashamed when we are misaligned with Him. There is a mismatch between what we are and what we are meant to be, just as if I were unfaithful to my wife and disowned my children.

When our high status as God's holy children is compromised by how we live and is contradicted by how we behave, then we need to be challenged and encouraged to shape up to our high calling by our friends and those who lead us. One way they do this is by appealing to both our sense of honor and our sense of shame. These belong together and work best in tandem. An appeal to our honor needs to be matched by the right kind of rebuke that "shames" us with its criticism of what we are doing or failing to do. Paul models this fine art well for us in his letters by combining honest affirmation of what is honorable with respectful censure of what is shameful.

Paul appeals to his hearers to show the right sense of shame with his use of a verb that refers to what is fitting or unfitting, proper or improper for them as God's holy people. Thus he maintains that it is "fitting" for women to dress and act modestly for devout participation in the Divine Service (1 Timothy 2:10). He urges his young fellow pastor Titus to speak respectfully to the members of congregations that he gathers in Crete and provide "fitting" instruction for them in their relationship with God and one another (Titus 2:1); he is to teach "sound, healing doctrine" with "healthy speech" that shames his opponents and gives them no reason to slander him (2:8). He also tells the Christians in Ephesus quite bluntly that it is not "fitting" for them as saints to engage physically or verbally in sexual misbehavior and abuse (Ephesians 5:3–4). It is, or at least should be, out of the question for them.

Paul also censures them by invoking their sense of shame. He "shames" them, kindly and respectfully, to encourage them to be the people they were called to be. He uses a different Greek verb to do this than when he usually speaks about shaming and being shamed.[117] It is significant that this verb is also used for treating someone with due respect (Luke 18:2, 4; 20:13). Thus the author of Hebrews uses it for the respect that children rightly have had for the fathers who disciplined them (12:9).

---

117 The verb is ἐντρέπω, with its noun ἐντροπή (see 1 Corinthians 4:14).

Paul uses this verb for a respectful kind of shaming that lifts people up without putting them down. It does not attack the person but censures his or her shortcoming. So, on the one hand, Paul encourages Titus to set such a good example as a pastor that he would put his opponents to shame, because they would have nothing bad to say about him and Paul (Titus 2:8). On the other hand, Paul tells the Christians in Corinth that he does not even seek to "shame" them by comparing himself to them but to admonish them, like a father with his dear children (1 Corinthians 4:14. He does, however, "shame" them for lawsuits of some members against others (6:5) as well as for the denial of the resurrection of the body by some of them (15:34). In 2 Thessalonians 3:14–15, Paul decrees that the members of that church are to shame any lazy person who refuses to work for a living by dissociating themselves from that person. Paul qualifies this judgment with a telling remark: They are not to regard such a person "as an enemy, but warn him as a brother" in Christ. That, no doubt, applies to all such cases.

Like a small dose of a potentially dangerous medicine by a doctor, the proper use of shame is a fine art that requires great spiritual wisdom. It employs salty speech to admonish holy people to live up to their high calling. It is not punitive and destructive but restorative and constructive. It does not just focus on right behavior but is concerned with personal integrity. It affirms our God-given identity, fosters our true sense of worth, and protects our spiritual status as saints. It is therefore very beneficial for life in the church as the royal family of God.

Ugly Sexual Speech

Another kind of abusive speech is now quite common in our society, so common that it is barely noticed and seldom criticized. In fact, it is often regarded as a harmless form of emphatic self-expression. But it is really quite hurtful and harmful. I refer to the use of obscene sexual terms and crude sexual scenarios to shame people. This kind of verbal abuse plays on our all-too-human sense of embarrassment about our sexuality and our fear of sexual inadequacy, with its consequent uncertainty and vulnerability.

This kind of abuse of sexual speech comes in many guises, ranging from sexual innuendo and banter to the exercise of lewd and suggestive humor to embarrass others. It includes mocking the gender and sexuality of people and the use of crude terms for male and female sexual organs to belittle people personally by regarding them as nothing more than their genitals. Even worse than that, they curse them by saying that they should be sexually violated. Such speech degrades people of their worth by disparaging their sexuality. It treats something that is in itself clean as if it were dirty. It considers something that is holy for a Christian as if it were rejected by God as disgusting and shameful. It debases what is good and desecrates what is godly. It attacks the sexual identity of people and dishonors them as men and women who have been made in God's image. This exercise of sexual disparagement seeks to turn our proper sexual delight and enjoyment into disgust with ourselves and sexual repugnance at our bodies. It is all too often triggered by sexual disgust and arouses sexual disgust.

In Ephesians 5:3–4, Paul has this to say about the origin of sexually abusive speech and the remedy for it:

> 3But sexual immorality[118] and all impurity or lust[119] must not even be named among you, as is proper among saints. 4Let there be no shamefulness[120] or foolish talk or crude joking,[121] which are out of place, but instead let there be thanksgiving. (author's translation)[122]

Here, Paul tackles the issue of sexually abusive speech by connecting it with sexual immorality and the sexual impurity that is caused by lust. He traces this strange verbal behavior back to pornographic sexual lust that pollutes the soul of a person and results in sexual intercourse apart from marriage. The desire for forbidden sexual intercourse pollutes the heart of those who dwell on it imaginatively. Their inner impurity comes out in the open through the mouth with three kinds of lewd speech: speech that is openly shameful, speech that is insensitively foolish, and speech that is coarsely humorous. This last kind of speech does not show its true face but hides it behind the mask of witty sophistication and crude joking.

Paul rejects these three kinds of abusive sexual speech. They may be acceptable to unbelievers, but they are out of place with God's people because they are saints. They desecrate the holiness of the church as God's holy temple, the place where God resides with His people, with their bodies as holy shrines. Yet Paul's prohibition

118 Or "fornication." This is the term in the New Testament for sexual intercourse apart from marriage.

119 The ESV has "covetousness."

120 The ESV has "filthiness."

121 The three words that are used here are general euphemistic terms by which Paul hints at what he assumes are well known to his hearers.

122 For a helpful examination of these verses, see Thomas M. Winger, *Ephesians*, Concordia Commentary (Concordia Publishing House, 2015), 551–55.

of sexually abusive speech should not be taken as the rejection of people's sexuality and God's gift of sexual enjoyment in marriage. Crude sexual banter that is so common among those who have been sexually disappointed and frustrated should be replaced by the exercise of thanksgiving—thanksgiving to God for the gift of marriage as the sexual union of a man and woman as well as thanksgiving of a wife or husband to her or his spouse for the gift of sexual intercourse and its enjoyment.

A Watch for My Mouth

Remarks that affect our self-esteem make an indelible impression on us. I know that from my own experience, and I have seen it even more often from what has happened to people I know. On the one hand, I have forgotten most of what other people have said about me. But I have not forgotten the words that they have said to blame and shame me. Those words still haunt me and stain my relationship with the people who spoke them. Like fragile scars, they never seem to be completely healed, but are all too easily scratched open again by every new real or imagined slight. Unless I check myself, they still alarm me and anger me. On the other hand, I have also never forgotten the words that have affirmed and encouraged me, the words that rightly complimented and praised me. When I am low and feel bad about myself, these words come back to me to sustain me.

I also know from my own experience as a Christian and a pastor how the devil uses what people say to disparage and discredit us. But I also know how much good is done by words of grace that comfort and encourage, unshame and sustain us. And that has taught me to be careful with what I say and how I speak. That has been confirmed for me again and again by Luther's helpful explanation of the Eighth Commandment in the Small Catechism:

> We should fear and love God so that we do not tell lies about our neighbor, betray him, slander him, or hurt his reputation, but defend him, speak well of him, and explain everything in the kindest way.

When I was young, my father often told me to watch my tongue. And he had good reason to do so, because I had a quick temper and a sharp tongue. My mother-in-law used to admonish my wife and her sister to say nothing about others unless they had something good to say about them. Like these wise parents, James (in 1:26) warns us about the danger of unbridled tongues. This vivid figure of speech compares us to untamed horses that do not do what they are meant to do or go where they are supposed to go because they have not been tamed and are not checked with a bridle. Later, James tells us that our whole body needs to be steered by a bridle that is put on our tongues so that we do what we are meant to do. The problem is, he admits, that just as a horse cannot tame itself, so we cannot tame ourselves, let alone our tongues (3:1–8).

Let me explain this illustration, which may be unfamiliar to those of you who have never worked with horses. A bridle is the apparatus that is placed on the head of a horse by its rider. It holds a small piece of steel called a bit, which is put over the tongue in the sensitive mouth of the horse. Reins are attached to the bit to steer it and the horse, and blinders are placed beside both eyes to keep the horse looking forward without any distractions. After the horse has been tamed, the bridle connects the horse with its rider. In fact, it keeps the horse in such close touch with its rider that the two operate in a perfect partnership with each other. Like a horse with its rider, we are steered by Jesus. He tames our tongues and watches over them so that we obey Him by what we do and say.

Where, then, does this leave me? I know that I must guard my tongue so that I do not damage others but befriend them instead. Yet that is not easy at all. It goes against the grain. Jesus therefore calls me to pray to Him for help to watch my tongue. In fact, I need Him to set a watch for my tongue, as my own worst enemy, so that I do not shame those who shame me. In the words in the service of Evening Prayer (which are from Psalm 141), I do well to take refuge in Jesus at the end of each day and pray:

> O Lord, I call to You; come to me quickly;
> hear my voice when I cry to You.
> Let my prayer rise before You as incense,
> the lifting up of my hands as the evening sacrifice.
> Set a watch before my mouth, O Lord,
> and guard the door of my lips.
> Let not my heart incline to any evil thing;
> let me not be occupied in wickedness with evildoers.
> But my eyes are turned to You, O God;
> in You I take refuge.
> Strip me not of my life.[123]

123 *LSB*, p. 246.

Questions for Reflection and Discussion

1. Is there anything in this chapter that you would like to discuss?

2. Why is there so much teaching in the Bible on abusive speech?

3. What kinds of abusive speech have shamed you most?

4. Discuss the worst effects of abusive speech and Christ's remedy for the fallout from those effects.

5. How does the devil use our reaction from verbal abuse to get a hold on us?

6. Which kinds of gracious speech have helped you most to overcome the shame of verbal abuse?

CHAPTER EIGHT

Our Hope of Glory

It was fitting that He, for whom and by whom all things exist, in bringing many sons to glory, should make the founder of their salvation perfect through suffering. . . . That is why He is not ashamed to call them brothers.

(Hebrews 2:10–11)

"It has been a long, slow journey!" That is what a woman once told me. She had had a rather difficult childhood. Her mother had been unmarried, and she had grown up without a father. In fact, she never knew anything about her biological father, not even his name. Her mother's acceptance and love for her had been rather fickle, depending on how she felt about herself as a woman from day to day and how much she happened to feel the need to be appreciated and loved. But bad had turned to worse in the woman's adolescence when she had been sexually molested by her older brother. In her teens, she had left home and entered into a disastrous affair with a married man as a substitute for the father she had never had. But that affair only added guilt to her shame and left her even more confused and uncertain about herself.

In her late teens, she had gotten to know a young man who simply loved her without taking any advantage of her. To her amazement, he married her. He covered her shame with his love and showed his unconditional approval of her as a woman and his wife. He gave her a new stable identity with a new father and new mother and a new brother and two new sisters, who simply accepted her and loved her. That changed her, but not immediately. Whenever she was unsettled by some mishap, she was once again undone by a sense of shame and self-disparagement, which made her feel that she was useless, worthless, and unlovable. Yet despite that—and in fact, through all that—the pain of her shame gradually eased, and she gained a true sense of her worth as a person from her life in her new family. Even though her experience of shame still left its mark on her, she at least had some relief from it and the hope for eventual release from it.

Shame seems to leave an almost indelible, long-lasting imprint on us. It colors how we regard ourselves and others. Even the lightest slights leave their stain on us, whether they are real or just imagined. But the deepest and most lasting hurt comes when we are shamed verbally and publicly by somebody close to us, like a parent or a teacher or a spouse. That kind of slight is seldom, if ever, forgotten, but is filed away in our hearts and minds together with all other slights. They are recorded in such detail that we can easily recall them, and they leave an abiding need for approval.

Because shame is so deep-seated and so closely connected with who we are, it cannot be rectified at one stroke with a single act, like guilt with an absolution. Its remedy involves a lifelong process of personal rehabilitation and reformation that is far more radical and comprehensive than the journey of the shamed woman I mentioned earlier. It involves a spiritual death of the old self and the creation of a new self with a new life on a new basis with the hope for a new identity and a new sense of worth. That hope is based on the assurance Jesus made just before His death that He would share His glory with His disciples through their union with Him and one another (see John 17). The nature and power of that hope is what I now want to discuss in this final chapter.

The Quest for Glory Rather Than Fame

The threat of shame and the devastating fallout from it impels people to pursue fame. It is not enough for them to be as good as their peers; they must be better than them. They therefore fall prey to the lure of "empty glory" (author's translation). Paul uses that evocative term in Philippians 2:3 to describe the reason for self-promotion that drives people to prove that they are better than others. They try to lift themselves up by putting others down. They promote themselves at the expense of their rivals, because they fancy that their worth depends on their fame. Lose that and they become nobodies.

Yet the quest for fame is little more than the pursuit of empty glory because it fails to deliver what it promises. Those who pursue it and put their hope in it are put to shame by their faith in it. Despite its glossy veneer, fame is empty. It is empty because it is so fickle, finite, and ephemeral. It is fickle because it depends on the whim of fashionable public opinion rather than reality. It is finite because it is based on comparison with others. Thus the fame of a woman for her beauty disappears when she is outdone by another woman who seems to be more attractive. It is ephemeral because it does not last long, like the beauty of a woman that fades as she ages. Yet its emptiness does not at all diminish the quest for fame. In fact, it seems to galvanize it because it gives people something desirable to hope for and work for. It makes the world go round for them because they do not want to be insignificant and unnoticed, disregarded and overlooked. They pursue fame to gain recognition and admiration. They hope that fame will overcome the threat of shame and protect them from it.

The lure of fame does not disappear when people become disciples of Jesus and members of God's family. There, however, it takes on a different, more superficially acceptable focus, with the quest for spiritual superiority in the guise of spiritual excellence. The three Synoptic Gospels—Matthew, Mark, and Luke—report its repeated occurrence even among the twelve apostles in some detail to emphasize its persistence.

On the first occasion, the twelve disciples are arguing amongst themselves about who is the greatest of them (Matthew 18:1–4; Mark 9:33–37). Significantly, this happens after the transfiguration of Jesus and His first prediction of His death and resurrection. He undermines their vehement argument in an unexpected way. He does not reject their desire for greatness but refocuses it by teaching them two lessons. First, He asserts that anyone who wishes to be the first and greatest of them should become the last and least of them by becoming the "minister" of the whole community.[124] Then Jesus takes a little child into the center of the gathering, embraces him in His arms, and tells the crowd, "Whoever receives one such child in My name receives Me, and whoever receives Me, receives not Me but Him who sent Me" (Mark 9:37). Thus, He shows that in God's family the status of its members does not come from their position of importance and power in the family but from regarding the least important as equal in status to Jesus as God's Son.

The second occasion came later, near the end of Jesus' ministry. Matthew and Mark locate this incident after the third and final prediction by Jesus of His death before His entry into Jerusalem (Matthew 20:20–28; Mark 10:35–45). In this instance, the mother of James and John asks Jesus to assign the two top positions beside Him to her sons in His glory (Mark 10:37), His kingdom (Matthew 20:21). She wants them to share in His status and power. Once again, Jesus does not rebuke her and her sons for their ambition to reign with Him but uses her request to teach them that they will come to reign with Him by drinking the cup of His suffering and being baptized into His death. Then He teaches the other ten, who—despite their indignation at James and John—were equally ambitious, that they will not reign with Him by lording their power and authority over others but by becoming His ministers to them all. What's more, whoever of them wanted to be the greatest minister had to become the "slave" of the whole community; they would have to work hard for nothing but their living and "minister" by

124 The word that is translated in Mark 9:35 as "servant" is not the term for a "slave" (δοῦλος) but a "minister" (διάκονος) who helps and assists others in what they do.

giving themselves to others, just as Jesus was about to give His life as a ransom for all people.

The report of the third occasion, in Luke 22:24–27, came at the climax of the earthly ministry of Jesus, immediately after He had instituted His Holy Supper. No sooner had He done that than His twelve apostles again get into an argument about which of them is the greatest. Jesus repeats what He had said earlier and applies it to the role of leadership. Then He, rather pointedly, turns their attention away from themselves and their importance by asking them this rhetorical question: "Who is the greater, the one who reclines at table, or the one who ministers?" He answers it for them and everyone in their society with a second query: "Is it not the one who reclines at table?" Then comes the punch line that turns their notions of greatness on its head: "But I am among you as the one who ministers" (author's translations). Just as Jesus was present with His disciples at the Last Supper as their host and their waiter, so at every subsequent celebration of His Holy Supper, He will be with His disciples as their hidden host and waiter who serves them with His body and blood as their food and drink. In that way, He shows His true greatness as well as their greatness as His disciples. They sit with Him at His table because they are His courtiers who also reign with Him in His kingdom. There, we too share in His hidden glory on earth as His guests and ministers who serve others together with Him. There, the vain quest for empty glory is displaced and replaced by true glory, the glory of humility and self-sacrifice.

Boasting of Vindication

The burden of shame impels shamed people to pursue self-justification. Since their sense of worth has been damaged and their honor has been violated, they try to regain it by proving their worth to others and to themselves. They do that too in their relationship with God. They angle for vindication by Him with their good works, their moral and spiritual achievements. They commend themselves to Him in a favorable light3/4 task completed because they want Him to lift the weight of shame and exonerate them.

That quest for vindication motivates them in their boasting, with its claim to fame. Paul discusses this common practice of verbal self-promotion in his letters to the churches. There, the boasting was just as rife in the churches as it was in their social context. But unlike his pagan counterparts, who usually regarded boasting as a vulgar display of bad manners by windbags and nothing more than that, Paul regards boasting as the symptom of something far deeper. Socially, it disclosed the human need for personal recognition and approval; spiritually, it came from the urge for self-justification with God. That, for him, is the heart of the matter.

That's why Paul does not moralize about boasting and rebuke his fellow believers for it. He does not even tell them to put an end to it. Rather, he teaches them that God has already put an end to their need for self-promotion through the death of His Son. Since God the Father justifies all those who have been undone by sin and are far from His glory, Paul dismisses their quest for self-justification by instead boasting about the righteousness and spiritual achievements of Jesus that God has conferred upon them (Romans 3:21–26). Since salvation is a gift from God—a gift of grace rather than a reward for works—none of them could boast of their spiritual superiority, let alone their spiritual status and worth (Ephesians 2:8). They had no reason to compare themselves with others or regard themselves as better than others, because all that they are and have is a gift from God.

In 1 Corinthians 1:22–31, Paul teaches us that our justification by God through faith in Jesus calls for a new kind of boasting that is closely associated with God's strange way of dealing with the normal human experience of social status and worth. People normally avoid the stigma of shame and gain their social status and importance from the wisdom that they get through their education and expertise, the power that they have acquired by what they have achieved, and the wealth that they have inherited by birth into a rich family or have accumulated from investments. These qualifications provide them with their credentials for a high position in society and a place in its ruling class. Through Jesus, God shames those who boast in their own worth and chooses those who otherwise have nothing to have much to boast of through their union with Jesus.

God sent His Son to rescue people from shame through His shameful death on the cross. Jesus goes the way of the cross, the way of divine folly rather than human wisdom, the way of divine weakness rather than human power, the way of divine lowliness rather than human glory. Through the death of His Son on the cross, God debunks the human quest for fame. He deliberately chooses those who are regarded as nobodies in human society and calls them to follow His Son on the way by which He leads them through shame to glory. He makes Christ everything for those who are otherwise regarded as worthless and insignificant. He unites them with His crucified and risen Son so that they are vindicated by Him with His righteousness, made holy by Him with His holiness, and delivered from shame by Him as their Redeemer.

The disciples of Jesus, therefore, have something better to boast about from their union with Jesus than the fame that comes from human wisdom and power. In Him as their Redeemer, they have everything that is His as God's Son: God's wisdom, God's righteousness, God's holiness. These are gifts from Him for them to enjoy and employ. So Paul boasts in Jesus as his Lord (Romans 5:11; 2 Corinthians 10:17–18; Philippians 3:3). He even boasts in his own weakness because Christ's power is made perfect in his weakness (2 Corinthians 11:30; 12:5, 9–10). In fact, he boasts of nothing except the cross of the Lord Jesus and his creation as a new person through Him (Galatians 6:14–15). He boasts in his vindication by Jesus through His death on the cross.

We then have no need to seek fame and boast of our worth with God. But we can boast because He has already given us supernatural worth through our union with Jesus. His great worth as God and man gives us our worth. We are, in fact, worth the holy, precious blood that He paid for our redemption from shame by His death on the cross.

The Hope of Glory

Shame has many different causes and consequences. It is not unleashed just by our experience of injustice but also by our failure to be as we are meant to be—our failure to meet the expectations that we have for ourselves and the expectations that others have of us. But it goes beyond this and includes another little unacknowledged cause of shame, with its negative outcome. It comes from the failure of others to meet our expectations of them, such as when our spouse divorces us or our children let us down. In such cases, we are not just disappointed with them but we are also put to shame by them. Our misplaced trust and hope that we had put in them shakes us up and undermines our sense of worth.

We, sadly, are all too easily affected by that common kind of shame because we hope for so much from the people who are close to us and expect them to make up for what we lack. We expect them to love us wholeheartedly and give us their unconditional approval. We have such high hopes from them that they cannot but disappoint us. When they disappoint us, we give up on them and come down hard on ourselves for the failure of our relationship with them. In our hurt, we cover up our shame with cynicism and expect little or nothing from other people for fear of further failure. But deep down, we arc haunted by a sense of personal failure and diminished sense of our own worth.

We carry over that fear of shame by disappointment into our life in the church, where we are upset by Jesus, who seems to let us down by the troubles that we experience. Our troubles call into question our identity as children of God and our status as righteous and holy through faith in Jesus. We then feel that the hope that we have had in Jesus has disappointed us and will put us to shame. We feel foolish for trusting in Him and being misled by His promises.

In Romans 5:1–5, Paul shows us how God frees us from that kind of shame by taking us on an unexpected journey through trouble to glory. This is what he says about that way:

> *1*Therefore, since we have been justified by faith, we have
> peace with God through our Lord Jesus Christ. *2*Through
> Him we have also obtained access[125] by faith into this grace
> in which we stand, and we boast[126] in the hope of the glory
> of God. *3*Not only that, but we boast in our sufferings, know-
> ing that suffering[127] produces endurance,[128] *4*and endurance
> produces proven worth,[129] and proven worth produces hope,
> *5*and hope does not put us to shame, because God's love has
> been poured in our hearts through the Holy Spirit who has
> been given to us. (author's translation)

Here, Paul highlights five counterintuitive features of our journey to glory: our justification by faith, our ongoing access to God's grace through faith, our hope of glory, our suffering as preparation for glory, and our reception of God's love through the Holy Spirit.

---

125 See the use of "access" in Ephesians 2:18; 3:12.

126 ESV "rejoice."

127 Here the Greek word θλῖψις, which refers most literally to pressure, is a term for all kinds of affliction, distress, and trouble rather than just suffering from persecution.

128 In Greek, this word also refers to patience, persistence, and steadfastness.

129 This is my own translation of the Greek word δοκιμή instead of "character" in the ESV, which is how it is translated in the RSV as well as those translations that follow it. This noun is derived from the verb for testing something to prove its worth. Paul uses the noun in this sense in 2 Corinthians 8:2; 9:13; 13:3 as well as for the proven worth of what has been tested in 2 Corinthians 2:9 and Philippians 2:22.

First, the foundation for our deliverance from shame is our justification by faith in Jesus and His atonement for sin by His sacrificial death for us. We receive the Father's pardon for the sins that we have committed and freedom from the sins that have been committed against us. We are adopted as God's children and heirs. We have His approval and acceptance, His justification and vindication. We therefore have peace with God because He has reconciled us to Himself and is now as well pleased with us as He is with Jesus.

Second, through Jesus and His presence with us in the Divine Service, we have obtained access by faith into the grace in which we stand. When Paul speaks of our access to God the Father through faith, he compares us to the priests who had access to God and His grace at the temple in the Divine Service as well as to courtiers who stood before the king in his palace when they were on duty there. Yet we differ from them because our access to God the Father is not occasional but ongoing, together with Jesus, our High Priest and King. We have access to Him in His heavenly sanctuary. In that high position and place of honor, we now have access to His grace and favor for ourselves and others. We have access to His riches in prayer.

Third, we boast in the hope of the glory of God. We boast in the hope of God's glory because it is already, in some sense, ours. We boast in it because we already now have it in Jesus, who has been glorified for us. We therefore have the sure and certain hope of its full bestowal, which will happen when we are glorified with Him by our bodily resurrection and enthronement with Him in glory at the end of our journey on earth. We boast in that hope because we will not only receive glory from God but also share in God's own glory. What could be better than that! God the Father promises to share Himself and His glory with us.

Fourth, we also boast in our sufferings because in and through them our hope of glory is confirmed. They are not the goal of our journey but are an essential part of our preparation for glory. By our experience of trouble and suffering, God prepares us for glory by producing three things in us. Through suffering, He produces patient endurance that does not demand an immediate, complete, visible disclosure of His hidden glory as it waits for God to manifest His final purpose for us. Through our patient endurance, God produces our proven worth. He tests us and shapes our character so that we become increasingly receptive to Him and fit for life with Him. Through our proven worth that has stood the test of suffering, He produces hope. He debunks our self-deluding expectations and replaces them with true hope that corresponds with His high purpose for us rather than our desire for fame. He makes us fit for full entry into His glory.

Finally, the mark of the hope that God produces in us is that it does not put us to shame, as all other unreliable hopes so commonly do. The hope that has been tested by suffering does not let us down and will never disappoint us. It is based on our experience of God's love, the love that He has not just shown by the death of His Son for our justification; it is something we experience inwardly and personally in our hearts through the Holy Spirit, which God has given us and continues to give to us. God the Father pours His ever-flowing love into our hearts through His Holy Spirit's love to confirm our hope of glory because love is its sum and substance. God's glory is the glory of His love. He does not just love us; He Himself is love. The Holy Spirit convinces us of God's love for us, so that we know we will never be put to shame by God. His love is the essence of His hidden glory and our hidden glory in Christ. It gives us a preview of its full, visible manifestation to us and in us and through us.

That experience of the Father's love confirms our hope of glory, a hope that does not deceive us and put us to shame, even in our suffering. In fact, our suffering gives us reason to boast because it prepares us for fuller participation in God's glory, just as the experience of trouble by a married couple confirms and deepens their love. We can therefore join David with his prayer in Psalm 31:1: "In You, O Lord, do I take refuge; let me never be put to shame."

The Riches of Glory

Now that we come to the end of this book about what God has done to free us from shame, I want to conclude by considering what His goal is for us with our deliverance from shame. His goal is summed up in one word: glory.

We have seen how our experience of shame is closely connected with our identity. It has to do with who we are as people rather than the animals that we most closely resemble physically. We are shamed when our sense of worth as God's sons and daughters is called into question and undermined when we are treated unjustly by others as well as when we fail to be the people that we were meant to be or would like to be. We strive to overcome our shame by the quest for approval and vindication in the court of public opinion, the quest for public recognition that is all too often confused with fame. We try to gain public recognition of our worth by our self-promotion and self-justification. We rely on our achievements to prove our worth and compensate for our sense of shame. We climb the ladder of fame to gain importance.

But God takes us another way to a different goal. He came down to earth for us to bring His glory to us in our shame. Through the incarnation of His Son and His death, resurrection, and ascension, He adopts us as His children and brings us to glory together with Jesus. Through faith in Him, we share in His glory—the glory that covers us and dispels our shame, just as the light of the sun repels the darkness. It gives worth to those who feel worthless, hope to those who feel hopeless, strength to those who feel powerless, and love to those who feel unlovable.

Well, what is the glory that we have from God? It the worth that we receive through Jesus and His acknowledgment of us as His brothers and sisters. Through the incarnation of His Son, God the Father does not just restore our lost glory as people who were made in His image; He fulfills His original purpose for us by bringing us into glory through our union with His Son in His heavenly family, like the union of a wife with her husband's parents in marriage. Our union with Jesus as our brother is our union with His heavenly Father. We share in the sonship of Jesus as children of God. We share in His identity and status and divine life. His place with the Father is our place with Him. The Father's love for Him is His love for us, and the glory that He has from the Father He gives to us (John 17:24–26).

God the Father does not promise to make us famous, but He calls us to participate in His divine life already now here on earth. He calls us to share in His own kingship and glory through the Gospel of Jesus (1 Thessalonians 2:12). He calls us to share in His eternal glory through our union with Jesus Christ (1 Peter 5:10). That's why we can depend on Him to prepare us for that by keeping us firm when we waver; He will keep us strong in the face of suffering and grounded on Jesus. He calls us to obtain the glory of our Lord Jesus Christ (2 Thessalonians 2:13–14). So, just as Jesus took on our shame by His suffering and death on the cross, He now shares His glory with us here on earth.

Here we reach the limits of human perception and experience. Any teaching of it is a bit like trying to explain the radiance and beauty of light in black-and-white terms. Because we only get glimpses of God's heavenly glory here on earth, we need to explain its heavenly reality in earthly terms by comparing it to the very best that we know and by showing how His glory even surpasses that. We need to resort to the language of praise that resembles the most extravagant kind of boasting, praise that expresses our dazzled amazement and proclaims the excellent qualities of Him who called us out of the darkness into His marvelous light (1 Peter 2:9). Thus, in 2 Corinthians 4:17, Paul declares that God is preparing for us an eternal weight of glory beyond comparison, invisible glory that no eye has ever seen, no ear has ever heard, and no human heart has ever imagined, a hidden glory that God reveals to us by the Holy Spirit (1 Corinthians 2:9–10). All this comes from knowing the surpassing worth of Jesus through our participation in His death and resurrection (Philippians 3:8–11).

In this world, people gain fame from their wealth and the power that it gives them. Paul counters this by speaking about the glory that we receive from the spiritual riches and power that God makes available to us through faith in Jesus. We have "the riches of His glory that He has prepared for those whom He has called in His mercy" (Romans 9:23–24, author's translation). In Ephesians 1:16–21, Paul unpacks what that is in his prayer for the Christians in Ephesus:

> [16]I do not cease to give thanks for you, remembering you in my prayers, [17]that the God of our Lord Jesus Christ, the Father of glory, may give you the Spirit of wisdom and revelation in the knowledge of Him, [18]having the eyes of your hearts enlightened,[130] that you may know what is the hope to which He has called you, what are the riches of His glorious inheritance in the saints, [19]and what is the immeasurable greatness of His power toward us who believe, according to the working of His great might [20]that He worked in Christ when He raised Him from the dead and seated Him at His right hand in the heavenly places, [21]far above all rule and authority and power and dominion, and above every name that is named, not only in this age but also in the one to come.

---

130 This can also be translated as "opened."

We discover our glory by God's gift of His Holy Spirit. He opened the eyes of our heart to discover the glory of the rich, heavenly inheritance that we have as coheirs with Jesus and the great power of God that enables us to trust in Him, hope in Him, and know His love, the same energizing power by which He raised Jesus from the dead and enthroned Him at His right-hand side in heaven, the power by which He has raised us from spiritual death and enthroned us with Jesus in heavenly glory.[131] In Ephesians 3:14–19, Paul connects the riches of God's glory with the dwelling of Christ in our hearts though faith as His earthly temple, so that by the power of His Spirit we may know His love that surpasses knowledge and be filled with all the fullness of God. In Colossians 1:27, he adds that the riches of God's glory are part of a mystery, the mystery of Christ's hidden presence among His holy people in the Divine Service and in them as His temple. His presence with them gives them their hope of glory. The riches of God's glory that are available to His people in Jesus supply all that they will ever need already now in this life (Philippians 4:19). So then, our glory is our identity as God's sons and daughters together with God's Son, our inheritance from Him as coheirs with Jesus, the presence of Jesus with us and dwelling in us, our empowerment by His Spirit, and the knowledge of Him and His love.

But all that is hidden from human sight, just as God's glory was hidden in a cloud for God's people on their journey to the Promised Land. It is obscured by our human ignorance, weakness, and blindness. Just as our life is hidden with Christ in God, so our

131 See also Ephesians 3:4–7.

glory is hidden from us now (Colossians 3:1–3). But when Christ appears at the end of our journey on earth, we too will appear with Him in glory (3:4).

Nevertheless, by faith in Jesus, we already now share in Christ's glory. We already have a preview of what we hope for. That hidden glory is disclosed to us by the Holy Spirit, who opens our spiritual eyes to see what is otherwise invisible to us. That preview lifts the burden of shame from us now and the threat of shame from us at the Last Judgment, when we will face God and His final assessment of us and our worth.

Meanwhile, we live in hope. We are sure of our identity as God's dear children as we wait for the full disclosure of our glory together with Jesus, when we will see Him face to face. In 1 John 2:28–3:3, John gives us this vivid account of what that means for us now and our hope of deliverance from shame:

> [28]And now, little children, abide in Him, so that when He appears we may have confidence and not shrink from Him in shame at His coming. . . . [3:1]See what kind of love the Father has given to us, that we should be called children of God; and so we are. The reason why the world does not know us is that it did not know Him. [2]Beloved, we are God's children now, and what we will be has not yet appeared; but we know that when He appears we shall be like Him, because we shall see Him as He is. [3]And everyone who thus hopes in Him purifies himself as He is pure.

Here, John gives us three practical instructions about our eventual deliverance from shame. First, we must remain united with Jesus, so that we may be able to face Him as our Judge with confidence and not be put to shame by our fear that God the Father will not recognize us as His children.

Second, the love that God the Father has lavished on us through His Son proves to us that we are His children already now. That is what He calls us. That is who we are. That gives us our eternal, unshakable identity. We can therefore face Him with boldness and confidence, without any fear that we are not good enough for life with Him. The proof of our worth is not just His love for us but also the kind of love He has for us. The same love that He has for Jesus is ours, and more. The love that impelled Him to sacrifice His one and only Son sets us free from guilt and shame.

Third, since God has not yet finished His work with us, we are not yet able to see ourselves as God sees us. But we need not let our sense of shame at our apparent failure to be pure and right and holy fill us with disgust and despair, self-accusation and self-condemnation, because we can be certain of one thing: when Christ appears, we shall be like Him because we shall see Him face to face and see ourselves as He sees us. We have that glory already now because we look to Him in faith and hope. By our hope in Him, Christ shares His purity with us. We have faces that are free from guilt and shame, faces that reflect His glory, like the face of Moses, as we see the hidden glory of God in the face of Jesus (2 Corinthians 4:6). So, as we by faith look at Him and listen to Him, we behold His glory with a clear conscience, and the Holy Spirit transforms us inwardly into Christ's likeness from one degree of glory to another (3:18). And that is the end of shame for us.

Down to Earth

If you are like me, you will have found Paul's teaching about the hope of glory and its riches mind-boggling and well beyond the reach of your imagination. What's more, you will still be puzzled by the complexity of shame and God's remedy for it. So I now want to conclude by bringing it all down to earth and putting it all as simply as possible.

Remember the woman that I mentioned at the beginning of this chapter and her remark about her long, slow journey from chronic shame? When I asked her what had helped her most to cope with the burden of shame, she hesitated and then said, "My husband's love! He stuck with me through thick and thin and put up with my bouts of self-disparagement; he was with me when I was in the pits of despair, joined me there, and suffered with me. He encouraged me to unload my shame on him, and he listened to me without judging me. He showed how much he loved me by giving himself to me when I had nothing to give him in return."

That's how Jesus helps us. He carries us along with Him and gives of Himself to us. He suffers with us and takes on our shame. His faithful love brings the hope of glory down to earth for us. It frees us from shame and despair. Just as He sacrificed Himself for us, He keeps giving Himself to us. He translates the Father's love for us into human terms and gives us a preview of what is in store for us. That's why Paul tells us in Romans 5:5: "Hope does not put us to shame, because God's love has been poured into our hearts through the Holy Spirit who has been given to us."

Through Jesus, God the Father pours His overflowing, never-failing love most obviously and helpfully into our hearts in Holy Communion. There, Jesus gives us His blood to drink and pours out His life-giving Holy Spirit into our hearts. There, we receive the blood of His new covenant with us, by which He commits Himself to us eternally in love and cleanses us from shame. There, He offers Himself to us for our redemption from shame. There, He shares Himself and all that He has as God's one and only Son with us as coheirs with Him: His righteousness, His holiness, and His glory. There, He unites Himself with us and shares His Father's love with us.

In 1971, Gavin Bryars supervised a team that filmed a BBC documentary that recorded interactions with homeless men who were camped on the streets in central London. When he reviewed what had been recorded, he was surprised to discover one episode in which an old man said nothing but kept on singing a short song to himself over and over again. Bryars was so struck by the simple, heart-rending beauty of the song that he extracted it and issued it digitally. It has since gone viral in many different formats on the internet. This is what the man sang:

> Jesus' blood never failed me yet!
> This one thing I know,
> For He loves me so.
> Jesus' blood never failed me yet!

That was the man's remedy for shame. And I commend it as God's remedy to all of you who have been shamed. Remember that you, like everyone else, are worth the blood of Jesus.

Questions for Reflection and Discussion

1. Is there anything in this chapter that you would like to discuss?

2. How does divine glory differ from worldly fame?

3. How does God use our troubles to free us from shame and confirm our hope for glory?

4. How does the promise of heavenly glory already now help those who feel insignificant, worthless, powerless, hopeless, and unlovable because they have been badly shamed?

5. Why does God keep our glory hidden from us? How does He disclose it to us?

6. Which part of our promised glory gives you the greatest comfort and joy in your life?